Simply Delicious!

by Gertrude Wright

For years and years we've wondered where we could find those special recipes, that different touch that transforms a good meal into something absolutely elegant. Perhaps you have also wondered.

We knew there must be some place to find these "trade secrets" of the culinary world. There must be someone to tell how to make everyday meals more exciting, how to make entertaining more relaxing and rewarding, how to prepare that very unusual entree or that absolutely delicious dessert, and add that distinctive garnish.

Gertrude Wright is a widely respected cateress in the Midwest; and in this cookbook, she shares her knowledge gained through years of experience. It is with great pleasure and delight that we publish some of these proven "trade secrets" for special recipes, attractive touches, and secrets of how to make the difficult, easy.

We hope that you enjoy this very special addition to our Ideals Cookbook series.

ISBN 0-89542-636-6 295

IDEALS PUBLISHING CORP., MILWAUKEE, WIS. 53201
© COPYRIGHT MCMLXXVI, PRINTED AND BOUND IN U.S.A.

An *ideals* Publication

Second Printing

CONTENTS

APPETIZERS .... Page 3

BREADS, ROLLS AND KUCHENS .... Page 13

COOKING WITH EGGS .... Page 22

SALADS .... Page 28

MEAT .... Page 32

SEAFOOD .... Page 40

VEGETABLES .... Page 44

DESSERTS .... Page 47

COOKING FOR A CROWD .... Page 59

APPETIZERS

BRANDIED CHEESE SPREAD

- 2 c. Roquefort cheese, crumbled
- 1 c. butter
- ¼ c. brandy

Cream together the cheese and butter; add the brandy and blend until very smooth. Place in a covered jar and refrigerate until ready to use. May be served with Baked Toast or crackers, and can be kept for about three weeks.

HOT CRAB SPREAD

- 1 8-oz. pkg. cream cheese
- 1 T. milk
- 2 t. Worcestershire sauce
- 1 7½-oz. tin of drained, flaked crab meat
- 2 T. fresh green onions, chopped

Mix ingredients together and place in an 8-inch buttered casserole. Top with toasted slivered almonds. Bake at 350° for 15 minutes. Serve warm with crackers.

Pictured in photograph: Cocktail Prunes, Paté 'N' Miniature, Coconut Curry Balls, Individual Pizzas, Velveeta Cheese Strawberries and, center, Rose en Gelée.

CHEESE OVERS IN MINIATURE

- 4 oz. cream cheese
- ½ c. butter or margarine
- ½ t. salt
- 1 c. flour
- ½ lb. cheddar cheese
- 1 egg yolk

Cream together first three ingredients, then add flour and mix as a pastry. Roll the dough out quite thin and cut into 24 squares. Cut through each square diagonally, forming 48 triangles. Cut cheddar into 48 small pieces and place one in the center of each triangle. Brush edges with water and fold in half, pressing edges together with tines of a fork. Glaze top with a mixture of one egg yolk and 1 teaspoon water. Bake for 8 minutes at 425°. These may be frozen before baking; do not defrost before putting them in oven. Serve warm.

HORS D'OEUVRES PIE

- 2 1"-thick slices of rye bread, approximately 5" x 7"
- 3 hard-boiled eggs, finely chopped
- 2 T. mayonnaise
- ¼ t. onion salt
- 24 whole sardines
- 24 medium-sized shrimp
  Pimiento olives

Place each slice of bread on a large plate and cut into 12 pie-shaped wedges. Mix hard-boiled eggs with mayonnaise and onion salt and put mixture in pastry bag with star tube. Place a swirled edge around each pie-shaped wedge. Put a well-drained whole sardine in the center of each wedge and a shrimp on each edge, on top of egg swirl. Place a large swirl of the egg mixture in center of pie; top with a thick slice of pimiento olive. This pie is a very attractive centerpiece for a large appetizer tray.

Hors d'Oeuvres Pie

CHEESE STRAWS

¼ lb. cheddar cheese, grated
½ c. butter, softened
1 ¼ c. flour
¼ t. salt
Parmesan cheese

Cream together the cheese and butter; add dry ingredients and blend well. Chill in refrigerator; remove and roll pastry out quite thin. With a pastry wheel or sharp knife cut dough into twenty-four 1 x 6" pieces and sprinkle each with Parmesan cheese. Fold each strip in half lengthwise, twist each and place on buttered cookie sheet. Bake at 400° for 10 to 12 minutes. Can be kept for several days; reheat in oven before serving.

CREAM CHEESE PASTRY

Mix 3 ounces of cream cheese with ½ cup butter. Add 1 cup flour and ¼ teaspoon salt. Roll out as pie dough to line tin.

COCKTAIL PRUNES

1 lb. pitted prunes
¼ lb. pecans or water chestnuts
About ½ lb. bacon

Cook prunes until almost tender; remove and drain well on paper toweling. Slit lengthwise and fill each with ½ pecan or a wedge of water chestnut. Wrap each prune with a strip of bacon and secure with a toothpick. Brown in skillet, drain well, then refrigerate. Heat under broiler before serving.

These may be prepared the day before a party. I'm sure you'll find your guests wondering what's in these delightful hors d'oeuvres—most will be surprised to find they're eating prunes!

See photo p.3

ROSE EN GELÉE

In saucepan combine 1 tablespoon unflavored gelatin, ⅓ cup sugar and 1 cup water. Cook until the gelatin is dissolved. Add ½ cup cold water and cool. In the meantime, invert a fresh rose (which has been rinsed in water) in a small rounded bowl. Be sure to leave about 2 inches of the stem and a few leaves attached to the flower. Secure the rose with crisscross pieces of Scotch tape. Pour cooled gelatin mixture over the flower and refrigerate. When congealed, unmold on decorative plate or tray.

QUICHE LORRAINE

2 c. thinly sliced onions
3 T. butter
¼ t. pepper
Pinch of ginger
¼ t. nutmeg
2 T. caraway seeds
2 slightly beaten eggs
½ t. salt
1 c. sour cream
½ lb. bacon, diced
Cream Cheese Pastry

Sauté onions in butter until light in color. Fry bacon until crisp, drain well and set aside. Prepare cream cheese pastry (or any favorite type) and line pie tin. Mix onions with remaining ingredients (except bacon), and pour mixture into unbaked crust, sprinkling bacon bits on top. Bake at 450° for 10 minutes, reduce temperature to 350° and bake for 30 more minutes. Test with knife blade; if custard does not adhere to blade, the quiche is done. Six to eight servings.

CRAB SNACKS

1 8-oz. pkg. cream cheese
1 T. lemon juice
2 T. Worcestershire sauce
2 T. mayonnaise
1 small onion, grated
6 oz. chili sauce
1 7½-oz. tin of flaked crab meat
  Chopped parsley

Blend the first five ingredients together well and spread mixture on a pretty serving plate. Stir the chili sauce well and spread evenly over the cheese mixture. Top with crab meat and garnish all with chopped parsley. Serve with crackers or Baked Toast.

SMOKED TURKEY OR CHICKEN BALLS

1 c. cooked ground chicken or turkey
1 3-oz. pkg. cream cheese
1 T. sour cream
½ t. hickory-smoke salt
¼ c. grated Parmesan cheese

Blend first four ingredients and shape into 32 small balls. Roll each in Parmesan cheese, chill well and put a toothpick in each. Can be frozen.

INDIVIDUAL PIZZAS

1 6-oz. tin tomato paste
¼ t. oregano
¼ t. onion salt
1 3-oz. pkg. cream cheese
  Round crackers
  Anchovies, shrimp or sausage
  Parmesan cheese

Mix tomato paste with the oregano and onion salt. Place a dab of softened cream cheese on each cracker to prevent it from becoming soggy. Spoon a bit of the tomato paste mixture on cracker, then top with a rolled or flat anchovy, a large shrimp, or a piece of sausage. Sprinkle with Parmesan cheese and bake at 400° for 3 to 5 minutes. These can be prepared an hour or more in advance and popped into the oven just before serving.

See photo p.3

SESAME SALTIES

1½ c. flour
½ t. baking soda
½ t. salt
2½ T. shortening
¼ c. milk
2 T. vinegar
½ c. crisp rice cereal
2 T. sesame seed
1 egg yolk

Mix flour, baking soda and ¼ teaspoon salt with the shortening as you would for pie dough. Combine the milk and vinegar, then add to dough mixture all at once. Divide the dough into 36 pieces and roll each with your fingers into a stick 5 inches long. Brush each with egg wash made by mixing one egg yolk with one teaspoon of water. Sprinkle on topping made by mixing crushed rice cereal with salt and sesame seed. Bake at 425° for 10 to 12 minutes. Serve warm.

When instructions read "MIX AS PIE DOUGH" it is easiest to mix the ingredients with fingers or a pastry blender. The dough will remain fairly dry but pliable, with small balls of shortening visible.

HEN ON THE NEST

2 doz. hard-boiled eggs
¼ c. mayonnaise
  Whole cloves
  Pimiento

Peel eggs and cut them into halves. Remove yolks from 10 eggs; rice through sieve. Chop remainder of eggs and leftover whites finely, and mix with about ¼ cup of mayonnaise. Don't make this egg salad too soft, or it will not take shape. Place mixture in center of tray in a mound and shape into a hen with your hands, using a small amount for the head and the rest for a puffy body and tail. Sprinkle sieved egg yolk over the hen to resemble feathers. Use whole cloves for eyes, a long piece of pimiento for the comb and a tiny piece for the bill. Garnish the outer edge of tray with curly endive and surround with Small Hens On The Nest.

SMALL HENS ON THE NEST

- 6 hard boiled eggs
- 1 T. mayonnaise
  Dash salt and pepper
- 12 large shrimp
  About 1½ oz. cream cheese

Peel and cut eggs in half lengthwise, remove yolks and place through a sieve. Mix yolks with seasoning and mayonnaise; fill egg whites with this mixture. Put a large shrimp with rounded side down on top of each deviled egg. Notice how it resembles a hen in a nest? Tint a small amount of cream cheese pink and use a little for the bill, a swirl for each wing, and a bit for the tail. Place around the large hen with a tray of crackers.

Guaranteed to create a sensation!

PATÉ 'N' MINIATURE

1 envelope unflavored gelatin
1 10-oz. can beef consommé
  Pimiento olives
1 4½-oz. can liver paste
1 4½-oz. can deviled ham
1 4½-oz. pkg. cream cheese
1 t. finely chopped onion
  Crackers or toast rounds

Heat gelatin in consommé with 3 teaspoons of water until thoroughly dissolved; cool. Brush 24 tiny muffin tins with salad oil. Place 1 teaspoon of gelatin mixture in each tin along with one slice of pimiento olive. Allow to set. Blend the liver paste, deviled ham, cream cheese, and onion with ¼ cup of the dissolved gelatin mixture; spoon 1 tablespoon of this mixture over the olive slice in each muffin tin. Top with remainder of clear gelatin, spooning over each paté. Chill until firm. To unmold, loosen paté around outer edge with knife and carefully dip pan quickly in warm water. Invert pan. Place one mold on each cracker or toast round. These can be made a day in advance, but should not be unmolded until half an hour before serving. Very professional looking! Quantity . . . 24 Patés 'N' Miniature.

See photo p.3

LIVER PASTE

1 lb. chicken livers
½ t. baking soda
3 strips bacon
1 medium onion, chopped
2 T. mayonnaise

Soak chicken livers in cold water with baking soda. Drain well on paper toweling. Cover livers with slightly salted water and simmer until tender. Cool and drain, reserving about 2 tablespoons liquid. Dice the bacon and fry until crisp with the chopped onion. Drain and combine with mayonnaise, livers, and the reserved liver broth. Place all ingredients in blender and blend until smooth. Refrigerate the paste. Serve with thinly sliced rye bread, crackers or toast. Can be kept for several days when refrigerated.

CHEESIES

1½ c. grated Swiss cheese
¼ c. grated Parmesan cheese
½ c. butter or margarine
¾ c. flour
¾ t. salt
⅛ t. nutmeg
1 egg white
  Paprika

Mix cheese and softened butter together; add flour, salt and nutmeg; blend well. Chill for 15 minutes. Form into 60 small balls, place on buttered sheet, and flatten each with a fork. Brush with egg wash made by beating one egg white with 1 teaspoon of water. Bake at 425° for 10 minutes. Cool and sprinkle with paprika. Store in covered jar.

DEVILED HAM PUFFS

1 8-oz. pkg. cream cheese
¼ t. baking powder
¼ t. onion salt
1 egg yolk
1 4½-oz. tin deviled ham
  Crackers or Baked Toast

Mix all ingredients together well. Place in a pastry bag with large star tube and squeeze onto toast or crackers. (If pastry bag is not available, use a teaspoon and dab a small amount on each cracker.) Broil for 5 to 8 minutes or until puffy; serve immediately. These may be prepared in advance and refrigerated until ready to broil. Crackers might become soggy, but will become crisp again in the oven. Quantity . . . 20 to 24.

SAUERBRATEN MEATBALLS

Prepare your favorite type of meatball mixture, shaping into tiny balls. One pound of ground beef will produce 48 balls. Brown meatballs well in butter and serve with prepared sauce in chafing dish.

SAUERBRATEN SAUCE

1 medium onion, grated
1 T. butter
1¼ c. water
2 T. sugar
1 c. gingersnaps, crushed
½ t. salt
¼ c. vinegar
2 bay leaves
6 whole peppercorns

Sauté onion in butter until slightly browned. Add remaining ingredients and boil until slightly thickened. Strain and pour over meatballs. Sauce should be thick, but you may add water if desired.

STUFFED MUSHROOMS

1 lb. large fresh mushrooms
¼ c. butter
½ c. soft bread crumbs
1 c. coarsely chopped nuts
1 t. salt
1 T. catsup
4 strips of bacon
½ c. light cream or half-and-half

Wash mushrooms in salted water; drain and remove stems. Chop stems fine and sauté them in the butter for about 5 minutes. Combine with the bread crumbs, chopped nuts, salt and catsup, then stuff mushroom caps with mixture. Garnish with tiny strips of bacon placed crisscross on top of mushrooms. Arrange the filled caps in a pan and surround them with the cream. Bake at 400° for 25 minutes. Remove, and serve hot on crackers or baked toast. This recipe serves six guests and is delicious with a fresh fruit salad.

Sauerbraten Meatballs

Each day can be a holiday
Filled with festive cheer
If we add a touch of color there
And a fancy garnish here.
It only takes a little time
To spark a simple meal,
And give each ordinary dish
A wonderful appeal!

STRAWBERRY NOG

4 eggs, separated
2 c. light cream
½ c. sugar
2 10-oz. pkg. frozen strawberries, thawed
1 qt. milk
1 c. light rum

Beat egg yolks with the cream. Add ¼ c. sugar, strawberries, milk and rum. Beat the four egg whites until fluffy but not dry. Carefully add ¼ cup sugar to the egg whites, then fold both mixtures together. Serves 12. This nog is a delightful starter for a spring luncheon. It is a delicate pink color and very fluffy. To serve, pour into tall sherbet glasses, garnish with a fresh strawberry, and sprinkle grated nutmeg over the top.

WEDDING PUNCH

2 32-oz. bottles of white soda
6 c. Rhine wine
1 pt. orange or lemon sherbet

Pour wine and soda over ice in a large punch bowl. Fold in the sherbet and blend thoroughly with a large spoon. Serves about 20 guests.

PINEAPPLE FIZZ

12 oz. pineapple juice
2 eggs
¼ c. sugar
1 c. white rum

Beat ingredients together until frothy. Serve over ice in tall glasses. Quantity . . . 8 to 10 glasses.

CREAMY TOMATO COCKTAIL

1 cucumber
12 oz. V-8 juice
½ pt. sour cream
2 t. salt
2 T. grated onion
1 T. dry mustard

Peel cucumber, cut in half lengthwise and scrape out seeds. Grate on a fine grater and squeeze out juice. (Juice may be kept and used later in cooking vegetables, preparing salads, etc.) Add remaining ingredients to grated cucumber pulp, and mix in a blender. Serve over ice cubes in sherbet glasses. About 8 servings—delicious on a warm day.

> To give holiday cocktails a festive touch, dip the rim of each glass in lemon juice, then in red sugar. Attach a small piece of Christmas greens with a red ribbon to the stem of the glass.

RASPBERRY COCKTAIL

1 qt. raspberry sherbet
1 pt. light cream
12 jiggers (18 oz.) light or dark rum

Place in blender with a few ice cubes. Serves 12.

PARTY PINK CHAMPAGNE PUNCH

1 bottle (4/5 qt.) pink champagne
1 quart lemon sherbet

Combine champagne and sherbet. Stir well and serve in tall sherbet glasses. Garnish each drink with a fresh strawberry hung over the edge of the glass.

Photo opposite:
Wedding Punch

COCONUT CURRY BALLS

1 8-oz. pkg. cream cheese
3 T. sweet pickle relish
1 t. curry powder
   Salt
½ lb. toasted coconut

Combine all ingredients but the coconut; mix well. Form into 36 small balls, and roll each in toasted coconut. (Coconut can be toasted by placing it on a cookie sheet and baking it for about 15 minutes at 250°.) Refrigerate before serving. These can also be frozen; however, allow them to defrost for several hours.

See photo p.3

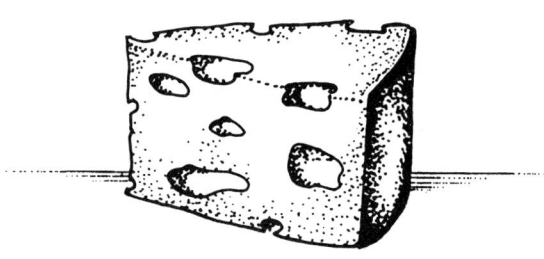

BAKED TOAST

1 c. butter or margarine, melted
8 slices of bread, crusts removed
   Poppy or sesame seeds (optional)

Press each slice of bread into melted butter, soaking thoroughly. Place on baking sheet and cut each piece into four triangles. Sprinkle with poppy or sesame seeds if desired. Bake at 300° for 30 minutes or until light brown. Cool at room temperature; store in a covered container.

These are delicious with dip, or used as bases for hors d'oeuvres of all kinds. Can be kept for several weeks.

CHEESE PUFFS

1 egg, separated
¼ lb. grated cheddar cheese
¼ t. baking powder
½ t. salt

Mix egg yolk, cheese, baking powder and salt. Beat egg white until very stiff, then gently fold in other ingredients. Put a small amount of mixture on cracker or toast, and place under broiler for 5 to 8 minutes or until puffy. Serve warm.

ORANGE SUGARED WALNUTS

½ c. frozen orange juice concentrate
1½ c. sugar
½ t. cinnamon
¼ t. cloves
1 T. grated orange rind
¼ lb. walnuts

Cook all ingredients (except walnuts) at a rapid boil for 2 to 5 minutes, or until mixture reaches the soft ball stage. Remove from heat and stir until it becomes cloudy. Add the walnuts and drop into mounds on a buttered sheet. Let cool at room temperature.

SPICED NUTS

½ c. sugar
½ t. salt
1 t. cinnamon
½ t. nutmeg
½ t. cloves
2 T. water
¼ lb. shelled halves of pecans or other nuts

Combine all ingredients except nuts; bring to a rapid boil and cook 2 to 5 minutes, or until a drop placed in cold water forms a soft ball. Remove and stir in nuts. Pour into well-buttered tin and cool at room temperature. Do not refrigerate these, as they will become sticky.

BREADS, ROLLS, AND KUCHENS

ORANGE CREME ROLLS

- 2 c. flour
- 2 t. baking powder
- ½ t. salt
- ¼ t. baking soda
- 1 c. sour cream
- ½ c. shortening
- 1 t. vanilla
- Ginger
- 1 egg yolk

Combine flour, baking powder, salt, baking soda, sour cream, shortening and vanilla, mixing as pie dough. Last, add a pinch of ginger. Roll dough out quite thin and cut into 1-x6-inch strips (makes about 36). Butter this number of clothespins; these will be used to wind the rolls. (See illustration.) Do not cover open end of clothespin, as they will remain in to bake. After winding the rolls, brush each with a wash made of egg yolk and water. If you wish, top rolls with a mixture of sugar and orange rind. Place on well-buttered cookie sheets and bake at 400° for 10 to 12 minutes. Immediately after removing from oven, carefully slide the clothespins out. Let cool, then fill with the following frosting.

Orange Frosting

Combine ½ cup butter, 1½ cups powdered sugar, 1 unbeaten egg white, 1 tablespoon orange juice and the grated rind of 1 orange. To fill rolls, place frosting in a paper cone and squeeze into center—much easier than using a knife.

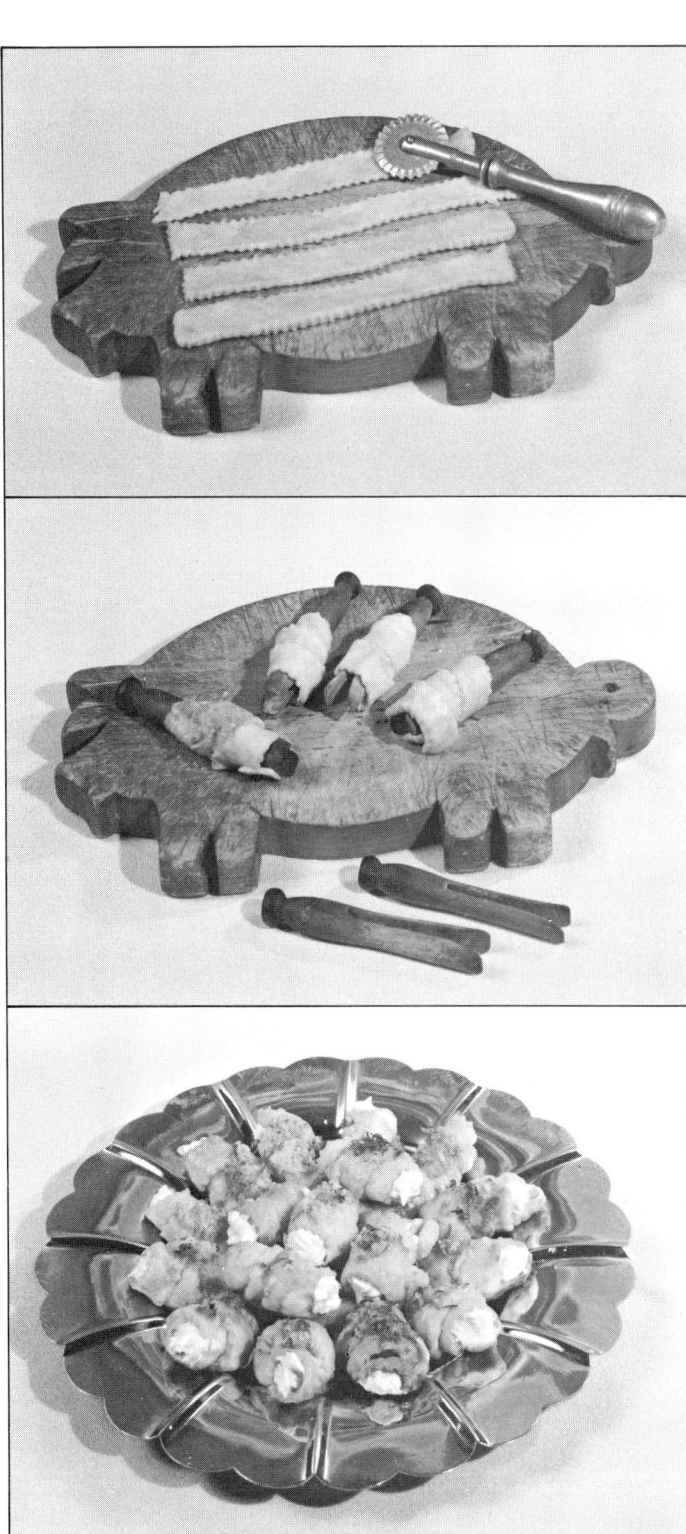

CINNAMON LOAF

1 oz. cake yeast
½ c. shortening
1 c. sugar
2 t. salt
3 egg yolks, well beaten
2 c. lukewarm milk
7 c. flour
½ c. melted butter
2 t. cinnamon
1 egg yolk

Dissolve yeast in ½ cup lukewarm water. Cream together the shortening and ½ cup sugar. Add to yeast mixture along with salt, egg yolks and milk. Add flour and beat ingredients well, then knead slightly and allow to rise until double in bulk. Divide dough into six parts and roll each part out into a long rectangle. Brush with the melted butter, then combine the remainder of the sugar with cinnamon and sprinkle some of this on each piece. Fold the outer edges of the dough together to form six long rolls. Place three rolls together and form a braid, pinching the dough together at top and bottom. Repeat with the other three rolls; place on buttered cookie sheets or in well-buttered tins. Brush with wash of one egg yolk mixed with 1 teaspoon water; sprinkle with more sugar and cinnamon. Bake at 350° for 45 minutes.

APPLE CAKE

½ c. butter
¼ c. sugar
2 eggs
¾ c. flour
¾ t. baking powder
1 t. vanilla
3-4 apples, peeled and sliced

Cream butter with the sugar; add eggs. Stir in flour, baking powder and vanilla; mix well. Spread one half of dough in 8" x 8" buttered pan. Cover with rows of apple slices, top with remainder of dough and spread as well as possible. Dough is soft and will cover apples while baking. Bake at 350° for 30 minutes. Cool and spread with a thin icing. Delicious served warm with ice cream.

Photo opposite:
Cinnamon Loaf, Butterhorns
and Mary's Filled Doughnuts, p. 16

MOTHER'S MUERBE TEIG OR BUTTER PASTRY

½ c. butter
1 c. flour
1 egg yolk
¼ t. salt
1 T. sugar
½ t. baking powder
2 c. fresh fruit, sliced
   (apples, peaches, berries)

Combine ingredients (except fruit) and mix as pie dough. Pat into well-buttered 8" x 8" tin. Top with fruit and sprinkle with streusel. Bake at 350° for 30 to 40 minutes.

STREUSEL

Mix with fingers, 1 cup sugar, 2 tablespoons flour, 1 teaspoon cinnamon and 2 tablespoons butter.

BUTTERHORNS OR NUTROLLS

1 oz. cake yeast
¾ c. + 2 T. sugar
1 c. butter, softened
2 c. flour
2 eggs, separated
1 t. vanilla
¼ c. chopped nuts
1 t. cinnamon

Dissolve yeast in ¼ cup warm water and 2 tablespoons sugar. Add flour, softened butter and a little salt; mix as pie dough. Add egg yolks, vanilla and ¼ cup sugar to the yeast mixture; mix well and divide into thirds. Roll each out into a long rectangle and cut each piece into 10 or 12 triangles. Make a filling with the egg whites, stiffly beaten, ½ cup sugar, the chopped nuts and cinnamon. Spread a teaspoonful on each triangle and roll up, placing each on buttered tin, point down. Don't allow to rise. Bake at 350° for 15 to 18 minutes and top with a thin icing.

ICING

Mix 1 cup of powdered sugar with 1 teaspoon hot water, ¼ teaspoon of vanilla, and ¼ teaspoon almond extract. Put on rolls while they are still warm for a shiny glaze.

FRENCH DOUGHNUTS OR SPRITZ-KRAPFEN

- 4 T. butter
- 2 c. flour
- 4 T. sugar
- ½ t. baking powder
- Rind of 1 lemon, grated
- 4 eggs
- Cooking oil

Heat 2 cups of water to boiling and dissolve butter. Add flour, sugar and baking powder and grated lemon rind; remove from heat and stir well. Add eggs one at a time, beating well after each addition. Place dough in a pastry bag with large star tube and press small circles of mixture onto buttered cookie sheet. Heat oil or fat in which to fry doughnuts. Dip a spatula into the hot fat, then gently lift a circle of dough and lower into hot fat to brown, frying about one minute on each side. Drain on paper toweling. When cool, ice or sprinkle with powdered sugar.

Hint: To sugar doughnuts, shake together in small plastic bag. Doughnut will be evenly sugared with no mess!

MARY'S FILLED DOUGHNUTS

- 2 oz. cake yeast
- 6 egg yolks, beaten
- ½ c. sugar
- 1 t. salt
- 1 c. butter
- 2 c. milk
- 6 c. flour
- 1 oz. brandy
- Prune filling or raspberry jam

Dissolve yeast in ¼ cup warm water. Add beaten egg yolks, sugar, salt, butter and milk; mix thoroughly. Add flour, then brandy (must be added last). Mix well; dough should be soft but not sticky. Refrigerate overnight. Remove and roll out to ½-inch thickness. Cut into 2-inch circles and, placing on palm of hand, press down to flatten. Place about a teaspoon of jam or filling in the center of each and fold sides over to center, enclosing filling. Place upside down on tin and allow to rise until doubled. Fry in deep fat, 2 minutes on each side. Remove and sprinkle with sugar. Quantity ... 5 to 6 dozen.

See photo p. 14

RUM KUCHEN

- 2 oz. cake yeast
- ½ c. milk, scalded and cooled
- 2¼ c. flour
- 1 t. vanilla
- ½ c. butter
- ½ c. sugar
- 3 eggs, well beaten
- 1 t. salt
- 1 t. grated lemon rind
- Rum glaze

Soften yeast in 2 tablespoons warm water. Add milk. Add ¼ cup flour and the vanilla. Cream butter and sugar; add eggs, salt, lemon rind and another cup of flour. Beat all ingredients together, adding the remaining 1 cup flour. Place in a well-buttered 6-cup ring mold and allow to rise until doubled. Bake at 350° for 30 minutes.

RUM GLAZE

Place ½ cup sugar and 1 cup water in saucepan. Allow to come to a boil so that sugar is dissolved. Add 1 tablespoon butter and 2 tablespoons light or dark rum. Spoon glaze over baked kuchen, making several small holes with knife to allow glaze to penetrate the cake. Kuchen may be frozen.

COFFEE KUCHEN

- ¾ c. butter
- 1⅓ c. sugar
- 2 eggs
- ¾ c. milk, scalded and cooled
- 2 oz. cake yeast
- ½ t. salt
- Rind of 1 lemon, grated
- ½ t. vanilla
- 4 c. flour
- 1 t. cinnamon

Cream together butter and 1 cup sugar. Add eggs and milk. Dissolve yeast in 2 tablespoons of warm water. Add salt, lemon peel, vanilla and 4 cups of flour. Combine with butter mixture and blend well; allow to rise until doubled. Pour dough into well-buttered 8" x 13" tin. Allow to rise again, then spread evenly with cooled melted butter (about 2 tablespoons). Sprinkle with remaining sugar and the cinnamon. Bake at 350° for 25 minutes.

MOTHER'S KRANZ OR WREATH

- 5 c. flour
- 1 t. salt
- 1 c. lukewarm milk
- 1½ oz. cake yeast
- 1 c. butter
- 1 t. vanilla
- Rind of ½ lemon, grated
- 4 eggs, separated
- ¾ c. sugar
- 12 oz. can of prepared filling (poppy seed, date, almond paste, cherry)

Dissolve yeast in milk. Mix 4 cups flour and salt; add milk-yeast mixture. Add butter, vanilla and grated lemon rind. Beat egg yolks with sugar; combine with other ingredients. Last, fold in stiffly beaten egg whites. Refrigerate overnight. In the morning, add remaining flour. (Dough should be soft but not sticky; a little more flour may be required.) Divide into three parts, rolling each out lengthwise until about 14 inches long. Spread each section with melted butter and the filling. Roll each lengthwise. Press these three long rolls together at the top and braid together, pressing together at the bottom again. Form into a ring. Place on buttered cookie sheet or in a well-buttered ring mold. Allow to rise. Bake at 350° for about 45 minutes. Top with a thin icing.

EASY DANISH KRINGLE

- 1½ oz. cake yeast
- ½ c. + 1 t. sugar
- 2 c. flour
- ½ t. salt
- ¾ c. butter
- 1 t. vanilla
- 3 egg yolks
- 1 12-oz. can prepared filling (poppyseed, date, almond paste)
- Streusel topping

Dissolve yeast in ¼ cup of warm water with 1 teaspoon sugar. Add 2 cups flour, ½ cup sugar, salt, vanilla, and butter; blend as pie crust. Add 2 unbeaten egg yolks and form into dough with hands. Divide dough in half and roll each piece into a long rectangle. Spread with melted butter and prepared filling (or fill with mixture of ½ cup sugar and 1 teaspoon cinnamon). Roll each piece lengthwise and place, open end down, on buttered tin. With a sharp knife, slit top of each long roll to 1" from either end. Brush with egg yolk wash, top with streusel and bake at 375° for 22 minutes. Top with thin icing.

STREUSEL

Mix with fingers 2 tablespoons butter, 2 tablespoons sugar, 1 teaspoon cinnamon and 4 tablespoons flour.

Mother's Kranz

MOTHER'S DEPRESSION FRUIT CAKE

1 c. shortening
1½ c. sugar
3¼ c. flour
1 t. cinnamon
½ t. cloves
1 c. juice of canned fruit
1 t. baking soda
1¼ c. glazed fruit
1 c. dates, chopped
1¼ c. nuts
1 egg, beaten
Hot Brandy Syrup

Cream shortening and sugar. Add 3 cups flour, cinnamon and cloves. Mix 1 cup glazed fruit, dates and 1 cup nuts with ¼ cup flour. Add baking soda to 1 cup hot syrup from canned fruit such as peaches or pears. Combine mixtures along with the beaten egg. Pour into 2 well-buttered bread tins and bake at 350° for 50 minutes. Top with additional glazed fruit and nuts. When cooled cover with the following syrup.

Hot Brandy Syrup

Boil ½ cup sugar and ½ cup water; add ¼ cup brandy or rum.

GRANDMA'S OATMEAL BREAD

2 oz. cake yeast
1 c. uncooked oatmeal
½ c. molasses
¼ c. shortening
1½ T. salt
1 egg
5-6 c. flour
1 egg yolk

Dissolve yeast in ¼ cup warm water. Bring 1½ cups of water to a boil, then add the oatmeal, molasses, shortening and salt. Allow to cool to lukewarm. Add dissolved yeast, one egg and flour to this mixture; beat well. Enough flour should be added so that dough is soft but not sticky. Let rise. Knead and shape into two loaves. Place in buttered tins, and allow to rise again until it is double in bulk. Spread top of each loaf with wash made by mixing egg yolk with one teaspoon water; sprinkle with a little dry oatmeal. Bake at 375° for 40 to 50 minutes.

ITALIAN BREAD

1 oz. cake yeast
2 t. salt
5 c. flour
1 T. salad oil
1 egg white
Sesame seeds

Dissolve yeast in 1¼ cups warm water. Add salt and flour, mix well, and knead for 10 minutes. Pour 1 tablespoon salad oil over dough and knead about 5 minutes longer, until dough is no longer sticky. Allow to rise until it is double in bulk. Divide dough into two parts and roll into oblongs, then shape into two long breads, each about 12" long. Using a scissors, cut several gashes across the top of each loaf. Place on buttered tin and brush the tops with egg white beaten with a fork in 1 tablespoon of water. Sprinkle each with sesame seeds and let rise until double (about 1 to 1½ hours). Bake for 10 minutes at 425°, then reduce heat to 375° and bake an additional 30 minutes at 375°. This recipe can also be made into four smaller loaves or eight individual loaves to be sliced at the table.

MOTHER'S KNAPF KUCHEN

3 eggs
¾ c. sugar
¾ c. butter
¼ t. salt
2 c. + 2 T. flour
2 t. baking powder
¾ c. milk
1 t. vanilla
Rind of 1 lemon, grated
¾ c. glazed fruit
2 T. slivered almonds
¼ c. powdered sugar

Beat eggs with ¾ cup sugar. Add butter, salt, 2 cups of flour, baking powder, milk, vanilla and lemon rind; stir. Last, add the glazed fruit mixed with 2 tablespoons flour. (This prevents fruit from settling to bottom of batter.) Sprinkle almonds in a well-buttered tube or kuchen or bundt pan. Pour batter into pan and bake at 350° for about 1 hour. On removal, spread with melted butter and sprinkle with the powdered sugar. This kuchen resembles a pound cake in texture and should be cut very thin. It can be frozen.

Photo opposite:
Caraway Bread, p. 20

EASY COCKTAIL ROLLS

1 oz. cake yeast
¾ c. milk, lukewarm
6 T. shortening
¼ c. sugar
1 t. salt
1 egg, beaten
About 4 c. flour

Dissolve yeast in 2 tablespoons warm water. Combine milk, shortening, sugar, and salt; add to dissolved yeast. Add the beaten egg and four or more cups of flour (dough should be soft but not sticky). Allow to rise, then shape into 48 tiny balls. Let rise until double. Bake at 400° for 10 to 12 minutes.

BRIOCHE ROLLS

1 oz. cake yeast
½ c. milk
½ c. butter
⅓ c. sugar
½ t. salt
1 egg, beaten
4 egg yolks, slightly beaten
3¼ c. flour

Dissolve yeast in ½ cup warm water. Scald milk and cool to lukewarm. Cream butter with sugar and salt; combine with milk and dissolved yeast. Add egg and 3 additional egg yolks. Then add flour and beat for 10 minutes. Cover dough and allow to rise in refrigerator until doubled (1-2 hours). Remove, stir down, and place on floured board, setting aside one fourth of the dough. Cut large piece into 18 pieces, form into balls, and place into well-buttered muffin tins. Form 18 balls from smaller piece of dough. Wet tops of large rolls with water and place small roll on top of each, pressing down a bit. Allow to rise until doubled, brush with wash made by beating egg yolk with water. Bake at 350° for 20 minutes. Rolls will be yellow in color.

CARAWAY BREAD

½ c. shortening
¾ c. sugar
1 egg, beaten
1 t. vanilla
¼ t. salt
1⅔ c. flour
1 T. baking powder
1 T. caraway seeds
¾ c. milk

Cream shortening and sugar together. Combine with egg, vanilla and salt. Combine dry ingredients and add to shortening mixture. Stir in milk and blend well, then pour mixture into well-buttered bread tin. Bake at 350° for 45 minutes to an hour. It is a good idea to bake this bread a day in advance for better slicing.

Top to bottom: Brioche Rolls, Baked Toast (p. 12) and Buttermilk Rolls

HARVEST ROLLS

2 oz. cake yeast
½ c. shortening
⅓ c. sugar
1 t. salt
¼ t. ginger
½ t. baking powder
¼ t. baking soda
½ c. warm mashed sweet potatoes
2 eggs, slightly beaten
4½ c. flour

Dissolve yeast in ¼ cup of warm water. Cream shortening and sugar; blend in salt, ginger, baking powder, and soda, mashed sweet potatoes and ¾ cup of warm water. Add yeast, eggs and flour; beat well. Knead for 5 minutes, then refrigerate dough for about 2 hours. Remove, shape into about 48 rolls and allow to rise again. Bake at 375° for 20 minutes. Rolls will be yellow, light and fluffy.

HARD ROLLS

1 oz. cake yeast
2 c. flour
1 T. oil
½ t. salt
1 egg white, slightly beaten

Dissolve yeast in 2 tablespoons warm water; add 6 more tablespoons of warm water, ½ cup flour, and 1 tablespoon oil. Beat well. Add remaining flour, salt and egg white to this mixture, then knead until smooth (about 5 minutes). Shape dough into a ball, place a little oil on top, and allow to rise until doubled. After rising, punch down dough and divide into quarters; allow dough to sit for about 10 minutes. Divide each quarter into three balls, cut a slit in the top of each and place on buttered tin about 2½ inches apart. Allow to rise until doubled, then bake at 450° for twenty minutes, with a large pan of boiling water on the bottom of the oven. This will produce a hard, crunchy crust but the inside will be soft—just like the rolls served in Europe.

DILLY BREAD

1 oz. cake yeast
1 c. creamed cottage cheese, small curd
2¼ c. flour
2 T. sugar
1 t. minced onion
2 T. dillseed
1 t. salt
¼ t. baking soda

Dissolve yeast in ¼ cup warm water. Heat the cottage cheese until lukewarm, then combine this with the dissolved yeast and the flour. Add remaining ingredients and beat well. Pour into well-buttered bread tin and allow to rise until double in bulk. Brush top with melted butter and sprinkle with salt. Bake at 350° for 40 to 45 minutes.

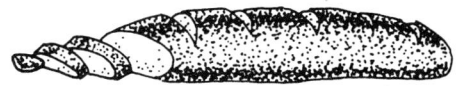

BUTTERMILK ROLLS

1 oz. cake yeast
3 T. sugar
¾ c. buttermilk, lukewarm
1 T. oil
2 c. flour
½ t. salt
⅛ t. powdered ginger
Melted butter

Dissolve yeast in ¼ cup warm water with 1 tablespoon sugar. Add buttermilk, oil and 1½ cups flour; mix well. Add remaining ½ cup flour and remaining ingredients (adding ginger last), knead well and refrigerate for at least 2 hours. Dough should be soft but not sticky. Remove and shape into 48 rolls; allow to rise until double. Bake at 375° for 12 to 15 minutes. Upon removing from oven, spread with melted butter.

# COOKING WITH EGGS

SHERRIED FRENCH TOAST

1 egg
1 c. milk
½ c. sherry wine
8 to 10 slices of dry bread

Beat egg and milk together; add sherry. Dip slices of bread in mixture and place on a buttered cookie sheet. Toast in the oven and serve warm with jam or syrup.

ALMOND APPLE PANCAKES

2 c. flour
¼ c. powdered sugar
¼ t. salt
5 eggs, well beaten
1 c. milk
2 T. melted butter
1 t. vanilla
1 #2 can sliced apples
½ c. toasted almonds
½ c. shredded coconut
Fruit Sauce

Mix flour, powdered sugar and salt; add to beaten eggs Combine with milk and melted butter. Make into thin, 5" pancakes and fry on both sides. Set aside on paper toweling while preparing filling.

APPLE FILLING

Add vanilla to contents of one #2 can of sliced apples; simmer about 10 minutes. Cool; add almonds and coconut. Stuff pancakes and roll them up. Place open edge down in a chafing dish. Top with sauce made of the juice of lemon, juice of 1 orange, 4 sugar cubes and ½ cup of butter. Heat until bubbly and pour over pancakes. Serve immediately.

THIN EGG PANCAKES—CREPES

4 eggs   1 c. flour
1 egg yolk   1 t. salt
¾ c. milk

Beat eggs, add milk and ¼ cup water and beat again. Add the flour and salt. Pour batter into a pitcher for convenience. Oil and heat a 5 or 6 inch skillet. Slowly pour about 1½ tablespoonfuls of the thin batter into hot skillet. Allow to brown quickly on high heat; with fingers turn crepe over to brown other side. Takes just an instant. Remove and place on paper toweling. Cool and fill or freeze for later use, separating individual crepes with foil. Quantity . . . about 30 small pancakes. Crepes may be filled with creamed chicken or with several asparagus spears, topped with a cheese or mushroom sauce. Or you might fill them with fresh raspberries or strawberries and whipped cream.

CHEESE FILLING

In blender combine six slices of bread (crusts removed), ⅔ cup of light cream, 1 teaspoon vanilla, 3 egg yolks, 3 tablespoons butter, 16 ounces of cream cheese and 1 tablespoon of grated orange rind. Blend until smooth. Top each crepe with one tablespoon of filling, roll up, place on buttered pan and bake at 450° for 4 to 5 minutes.

*Photo opposite:
German Apple Pancake
See p. 27*

MOTHER'S BREAD DUMPLINGS

1 egg
2 T. butter
½ t. salt
⅓ c. bread crumbs

Mix ingredients and shape into marble-sized balls. Drop into rapidly boiling water and cook for about 15 minutes. Add to hot soups or vegetables such as peas and carrots or kohlrabi. Quantity . . . about twelve ½" balls.

POPOVERS

2 eggs
1 c. flour
½ t. salt
1 c. milk

Beat ingredients together for only ½ minute. Fill well-buttered custard cups or iron gem pans half full. Bake at 400° for 30 minutes, then at 350° for 15 minutes. Do not open oven while popovers are baking. Makes 11 popovers.

CHEESE SOUFFLÉ

5 T. butter
5 T. flour
1½ c. milk
½ t. salt
6 eggs, separated
2 c. shredded cheddar cheese

Melt butter in saucepan; add flour, milk and salt, then cook until slightly thickened. Add well-beaten egg yolks and cook a little longer to incorporate eggs. Remove from heat and add the shredded cheese. Beat egg whites until peaks form; fold into other ingredients. Pour mixture into a well-buttered casserole. Place in a pan of water to steam and bake 1¼ hours at 300°. Serve immediately. Serves 4 to 6. For a spinach soufflé, substitute 1½ cups of cooked, chopped spinach instead of shredded cheese. Top with Parmesan cheese if desired.

Popovers

ROYAL CUSTARD

4 eggs, beaten
1 c. consommé or chicken stock
½ t. salt
   Pepper

Combine ingredients and pour into a buttered tin to ½" depth. Steam in a pan of water in a 350° oven until firm. Serve cubed in hot tomato soup or bouillon.

STEAMED APPLE DUMPLINGS

½ c. diced apple
¼ c. milk
2 T. sugar
1 t. lemon rind
1 T. butter
2 eggs, separated
1½ c. fine bread crumbs
   Wine Sauce

Combine apples, milk, sugar, lemon rind, butter, egg yolks and bread crumbs; stir well. Fold in stiffly beaten egg whites and shape into 6 large or 9 small balls. Drop into rapidly boiling salted water and cook for 10 minutes. Water must be boiling or dumplings will disintegrate.

WINE SAUCE

Mix 2 tablespoons of flour with ½ teaspoon of cinnamon, 2 tablespoons sugar, the grated rind of one lemon and one cup of dry white wine. Cool until thickened and serve hot over dumplings.

SOUFFLÉ PANCAKES

6 eggs, separated
1 T. melted butter
½ c. flour
½ c. sour cream

Beat egg yolks until very thick. Add the melted butter, then the flour and sour cream, alternately. Fold in the stiffly beaten egg whites. Drop mixture by tablespoonfuls on greased griddle. Brown, turning when top is bubbly.

FLUFFY OMELET SUPREME

8 eggs, separated
½ c. flour
¾ t. salt
   Pepper
½ t. cream of tartar
4 T. butter
¼ t. onion salt
1¼ c. milk
1 c. shredded cheddar cheese

Beat egg yolks with ¼ cup of flour and ¼ cup water. Add ½ teaspoon of salt and a little pepper; beat until thick and creamy. Beat the egg whites with cream of tartar until stiff but not dry. Fold egg yolk mixture gently into egg whites. Pile mixture into two well-buttered 8½" layer cake pans. Bake at 350° for 15 minutes. While omelet is baking, prepare cheese sauce. Melt butter in a double boiler. Add remaining ¼ cup of flour, ¼ teaspoon of salt, onion salt and milk; cook until slightly thickened. Add cheese and stir. Place 1 baked layer of the omelet on a serving plate and top with half of the cheese sauce. Place second layer on top and cover with remaining sauce. When serving, cut into wedges with 2 forks as it is very light. Serves 6.

VANILLA SOUFFLÉ

¼ c. butter   4 eggs, separated
¼ c. flour   1 t. vanilla
¼ t. salt   Brandy Sauce
1 c. milk

Melt butter; stir in flour and salt. Then add milk and cook until thickened; remove from heat. Add beaten egg yolks and the vanilla. Fold in stiffly beaten egg whites and place mixture in buttered and sugared straight-sided mold. Steam in pan of water in 425° oven for 22 minutes.

BRANDY SAUCE

Cream ½ cup of butter with 1 cup of powdered sugar. Add 1 egg and 2 tablespoons of brandy or rum. Mix thoroughly and serve with soufflé.

GERMAN APPLE PANCAKE

6 eggs, separated
¼ c. flour
¼ c. melted butter
¼ c. milk
½ t. salt
3 apples, sliced

Beat egg yolks; mix in flour, butter, milk and salt. Fold in the beaten egg whites. Heat 2 tablespoons butter in a large skillet; pour in batter. Top with apple slices. Cook over medium heat for about 5 minutes. Bake in 400° oven for 15 minutes until golden brown. Top with sugar and cinnamon.

See photo p. 23

APPLE OMELET

2 apples, peeled and sliced
6 T. butter
2 T. honey
2 eggs
Cinnamon and sugar

Cook apple slices with 4 tablespoons butter and honey for 10 minutes; set aside. Beat eggs with 1 tablespoon of water and pour into an omelet pan containing 2 tablespoons of melted butter. Cook without stirring until top is bubbly. Then lift mixture with a fork, from outside of pan to the center, allowing the liquid part to flow underneath. Continue cooking until set, then spoon cooled apple mixture on one half, sprinkle with a little cinnamon and sugar, fold over and flip on plate. For showmanship, heat ¼ cup brandy, pour over omelet and ignite. Serves two.

FLUFFY OMELET

2 T. butter   ¼ t. salt
6 eggs, separated   ¼ t. cream of tartar
3 T. flour

Heat butter in electric skillet at 300° for 10 minutes. Beat egg yolks with flour, 3 tablespoons water and salt. Beat the egg whites with cream of tartar until stiff. Fold the two mixtures together and pour into warmed skillet. Cover and bake for 10 minutes. May be served with fruit and sour cream. Serves 4 to 6.

BAKED EGGS

2 c. grated cheddar cheese
¼ c. butter
1 dozen eggs
2 c. light cream
1 t. prepared mustard
1 t. salt
  Pepper

Spread the grated cheese in bottom of a 9 x 13 x 2-inch pan. Dot with butter. Lightly whip the eggs; add the cream, prepared mustard and seasonings. Pour over the cheese and butter. Bake at 350° for 40 minutes. This is an easy way to prepare eggs for 8 guests at a brunch.

VELVEETA CHEESE GARNISHES

For strawberries, shape soft cheese into form of a strawberry, roll in red sugar, and top with a small sprig of parsley. Place in a paper bonbon cup if desired. Nice accompaniment for a fruit salad or dessert. To make cheese pumpkins, shape into balls, top each with an inverted clove for a stem and, using a toothpick dipped in yellow food coloring, make indentations around the sides. Use to top a torte or pumpkin pie.

Photo opposite:
Crisp Green Salad, p. 28

SALADS

CRISP GREEN SALAD

1 T. minced onion
¼ c. French dressing
¼ c. crumbled blue cheese
1 16-oz. can French cut green beans, drained
1 small tin anchovies
½ c. sour cream
1 head lettuce

Combine minced onion, dressing, blue cheese, and the green beans. Drain chilled anchovies, retaining 1 tablespoon of oil; chop, then add above ingredients to the sour cream. Last, add the head of lettuce torn into medium-size pieces. Toss, chill and serve. Serves 8.

LEMON MOLD

1 6-oz. pkg. lemon gelatin
1 8-oz. pkg. cream cheese
½ c. heavy cream, whipped
    Fresh fruit
    Rum Fruit Dressing

Dissolve gelatin in 2 cups boiling water; cool. Cream the cream cheese with ½ cup of the cooled gelatin. Add the whipped cream to the above ingredients, place in a well-oiled 4- to 6-cup ring mold and refrigerate. Unmold and serve surrounded with fresh fruits such as sugared whole strawberries, wedges of cantaloupe, watermelon chunks, small clusters of green grapes, or pieces of fresh pineapple.

RUM FRUIT DRESSING

½ c. heavy cream, whipped
16 large marshmallows, quartered
½ t. rum flavoring or 2 T. white rum
    A few drops of red or green food coloring

Serve in tall compote or in hollowed-out shell of a fresh pineapple for a decorative touch.

CHERRY SALAD

1 3½-oz. pkg. cherry gelatin
1 #2 can sour cherries
2 3-oz. pkg. cream cheese
    Chopped nuts

Dissolve gelatin in 1 cup hot water and 1 cup of juice drained from canned cherries, along with 2 cups of cherries. Form cream cheese into 8 balls; roll these in chopped nuts. Place each ball in an individual well-oiled mold. Cover with cooled gelatin mixture and refrigerate until set. Unmold and serve on individual beds of lettuce or curly endive. Serve with "Tang" dressing.

"TANG" DRESSING

Mix 1 cup sour cream with 2 teaspoons instant orange drink powder and 1-2 teaspoons sugar. Unusual and tart.

SEVEN LAYERED SALAD

1 head lettuce, shredded
1 green pepper, diced
1 c. chopped celery
1 large onion, chopped
1 16-oz. can peas, drained
2 c. mayonnaise
2 T. brown sugar
½ c. shredded cheddar cheese
½ c. crisp bacon bits

Prepare salad in a large bowl. Add ingredients one at a time as given, each in a separate layer. Do not toss. Cover and refrigerate for 8 hours or overnight. Serve in bowl, making sure each guest digs down deep to get a portion of each layer. You may also prepare in individual salad bowls, again making seven layers. This salad will keep one or two days if necessary. Makes 8 generous servings.

CHICKEN MOUSSE

1½ c. chicken stock *or* bouillon
½ t. salt
3 egg yolks, slightly beaten
1 envelope unflavored gelatin
3 c. diced cooked chicken
1½ t. horseradish
1¼ c. whipped cream

Heat chicken stock, salt, and egg yolks. Cover unflavored gelatin with 2 tablespoons water; add to heated broth and egg mixture until gelatin is dissolved. Cool. Fold in chicken, horseradish and whipped cream. Mold and chill.

SEA DREAM SALAD

6 oz. pkg. lime gelatin
1 t. salt
½ c. chopped onion
2 c. shredded cucumber

Dissolve gelatin in 2¼ cups of hot water. When partially congealed, whip until fluffy. Add salt, onion, cucumber and 4 tablespoons water. Mold and refrigerate. Serve surrounded with tomato wedges and thin slices of cucumber, and a sour cream dressing. Dressing suggestion: Combine 1 cup of sour cream with ½ teaspoon onion salt and 1 tablespoon chopped chives.

RICE MOLD

2 envelopes unflavored gelatin
2 cups cooked white rice
8 oz. cream cheese
¼ c. sugar
½ t. vanilla
½ t. almond extract
½ c. heavy cream, whipped

Soften gelatin in ¼ cup cold water. Add 2 cups hot water; stir until gelatin is dissolved. Add rice and cool. Cream the cream cheese with a little of the above mixture. Combine with remaining gelatin mixture, sugar, vanilla and almond extract. Last, fold in whipped cream and tint a delicate color if desired. Refrigerate in a six-cup mold. Serve surrounded with fresh fruits and Rum Fruit Dressing if you like. Serves 8.

CRAB MEAT MOLD

8 oz. cream cheese
1 10½-oz. can tomato soup
2 T. unflavored gelatin
2 c. diced celery
1 4½-oz. can crab meat, flaked
½ green pepper, finely chopped
1 small onion, finely chopped
4 hard-boiled eggs, chopped
1 c. mayonnaise

Melt the cream cheese in the undiluted tomato soup. Soften gelatin in ½ cup of cold water and add to the hot soup mixture. Add remaining ingredients, folding the cup of mayonnaise in last. Place in a well-oiled 6-cup ring mold and chill until set. Serve on greens with any type of dressing.

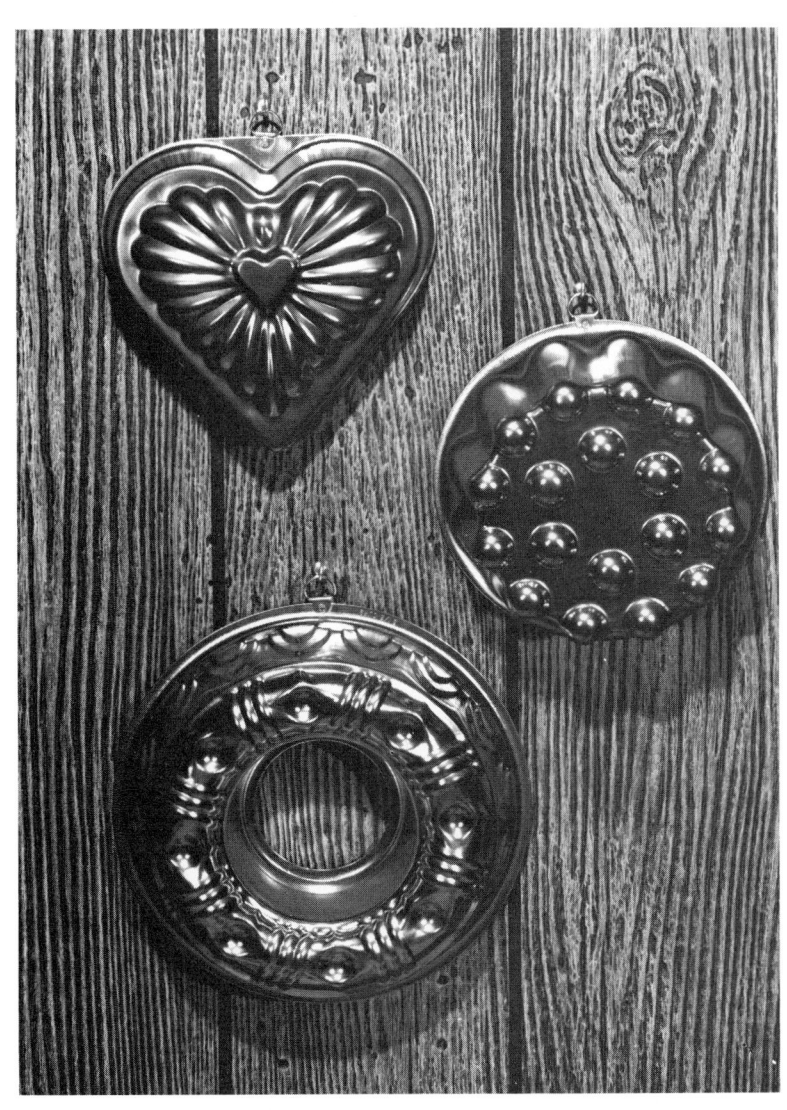

CARDINAL SALAD

- 2 3-oz. pkgs. lemon gelatin
- 2 3-oz. pkgs. strawberry gelatin
- 1 #2 can beets
- ¼ c. vinegar
- ½ t. salt
- 2 T. grated onion
- 2 T. horseradish
- 1 c. diced celery
- 2 c. chopped cabbage

Dissolve the 4 packages of gelatin with the juice from the canned beets combined with water to make 4½ cups. Chop the beets and add to gelatin along with remaining ingredients. Place in 8-cup ring mold; refrigerate. Serve with sour cream and garnish with greens.

MOLDED EGG SALAD

- 3 T. unflavored gelatin
- 1½ c. mayonnaise
- 3 T. lemon juice
- ½ t. salt
- 1 T. catsup
- 10 hard-boiled eggs, finely chopped
- 2 T. sweet pickle relish
- 2 T. chopped green pepper

Dissolve gelatin in ¼ cup cold water; add 1½ cups of boiling water and mayonnaise. Combine with remaining ingredients, then place in well-oiled ring mold and chill.

CRANBERRY MOLD

- 1 6-oz. pkg. lemon gelatin
- 1 c. sugar
- 2 apples, peeled and cored
- 2 oranges, peeled and sectioned
- 1 lb. fresh cranberries, chopped
- 3 oz. canned grated pineapple, drained

Dissolve gelatin in 2 cups hot water with 1 cup of sugar. When gelatin starts to congeal, add chopped apples, oranges and cranberries, along with pineapple. Place in 6-cup ring mold and refrigerate until set.

PARADISE CRANBERRY SALAD

- 1 lb. fresh cranberries
- ¼ c. sugar
- 1 c. seeded grapes
- 16 large marshmallows
- ½ c. drained maraschino cherries
- ½ c. heavy cream, whipped
- ½ c. chopped nuts

Chop or grind cranberries. Quarter marshmallows; cut grapes and cherries in half; combine fruit with sugar. Fold in whipped cream and nuts; refrigerate. Serve on lettuce or curly endive with a small dab of whipped cream on top. A lovely holiday innovation that goes well with poultry.

TWO-TONED CHRISTMAS SALAD

- 3 c. fresh cranberries
- 3 T. unflavored gelatin
- 2 c. sugar
- 1½ c. chicken broth
- 3 c. diced cooked chicken
- 1 t. salt
- ½ t. paprika
- 1 c. seeded grapes, halved
- ½ c. toasted almonds
- ½ c. mayonnaise
- ½ c. diced celery
- ¼ c. heavy cream, whipped

Dissolve 1 tablespoon unflavored gelatin in ½ cup cold water. Cook the cranberries in 1 cup of water until softened, about 15 minutes. Add gelatin and 2 cups of sugar to the hot berries. Pour mixture in the bottom of a well-oiled 6-cup ring mold; refrigerate. Dissolve 2 tablespoons gelatin in 1 cup of water. Add 1½ cups chicken broth and remaining ingredients; stir. Pour this mixture over the congealed cranberries in mold. Refrigerate. Unmold and serve on greens.

Photo opposite:
Beef Wellington, p. 32

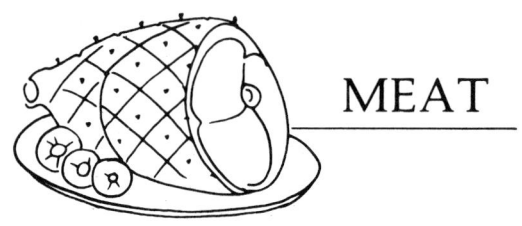# MEAT

BEEF WELLINGTON

1 3-lb. tenderloin
1 large onion, chopped fine
½ lb. fresh mushrooms, sliced
2 T. red wine
3 c. flour
1 c. shortening
¼ c. 7-Up
   Salt
1 egg yolk

Remove tail ends of tenderloin. Spread meat with melted butter, season well and refrigerate until butter has hardened. Remove and bake at 450° for 35 minutes. (Inside of meat will still be pink.) Chill well in refrigerator. In the meantime, prepare the filling: Sauté chopped onion and mushrooms in 4 tablespoons of butter. Add wine, stir well and cool. To prepare pastry, mix flour and shortening with the 7-Up and a little salt. Roll out to ¼" thickness. Place cooled filling lengthwise in center of pastry. Place chilled meat on top of filling and fold pastry over the meat, tucking ends of pastry under and sealing edges with a bit of water. Place on a well-buttered pan. Make small leaves and twisted flowers with leftover scraps of dough, and put on top with a bit of water. Brush entire pastry with an egg yolk beaten with 1 teaspoon water. Bake at 400° for 20 minutes or until golden brown.

FROSTED MEAT LOAF

2 lbs. ground beef
1 lb. ground veal
½ lb. ground ham or pork
2 eggs
2 c. soft bread crumbs
1½ t. salt
3 c. tomato juice
3 c. mashed potatoes
1 egg yolk

Combine all ingredients except mashed potatoes and egg yolk. Place in a well-buttered baking dish and bake at 350° for one hour. Drain off the juice and frost with the mashed potatoes. Brush with an egg yolk mixed with 1 tablespoon of water. Heat under broiler until slightly browned. Serves 10 to 12.

GROUND BEEF WELLINGTON

1½ lbs. ground sirloin or round steak
2 T. horseradish
1 t. salt
¼ c. melted butter
   One-half of filling and pastry used for Beef Wellington
   Sauce Supreme

Combine ground beef, horseradish, salt and a little pepper and shape into a loaf. Spread well with melted butter, then refrigerate until butter has hardened. Bake at 400° for 20 minutes; cool. Place filling on center of prepared dough and wrap as Beef Wellington. Bake at 375° for 20 minutes. Serve with the following sauce.

Sauce Supreme

Sauté 6 tablespoons of melted butter and brown. Add 4 tablespoons of flour, 1 cup light cream, a little salt and ½ cup of light wine. When serving, ½ cup of warmed brandy can be added to sauce and ignited. Serves 4.

SWEDISH MEATBALLS

- 2 lbs. ground beef
- 1½ c. fine bread crumbs
- 1 t. salt
- Pepper
- ¼ c. milk
- ¼ c. applesauce
- 2 eggs
- 1 t. minced onion
- ¼ t. nutmeg

Combine ingredients, mix well and form into 48 small balls. Brown in butter, then add water to simmer (about 2 cups). Cook, covered, for about 15 minutes. Serve over rice or noodles. These freeze very well and can also be made smaller to use as hors d'oeuvres.

OVEN STEW

- 4 potatoes
- 1 stalk celery
- 6 carrots
- 2 lbs. chuck beef, cut up
- 1 medium onion, sliced
- 2 t. salt
- 2 T. tapioca
- 1 T. sugar
- 1 c. tomato juice or wine
- 2 bay leaves

Quarter potatoes; cut celery and carrots into chunks. Place in a buttered baking dish with the meat and onion. Sprinkle with the salt, tapioca and sugar. Pour tomato juice or wine over stew and add bay leaves. Bake, covered, at 300° for four hours.

Oven Stew

STUFFED HAMBURGER SQUARES

- 1 lb. ground beef
- 1 t. salt
- ½ medium onion, minced
- 1 c. soft bread crumbs
- 1 egg, beaten
- 1 c. tomato juice
- 3 c. prepared seasoned stuffing mix
- 2 10½-oz. cans cream of mushroom soup, undiluted

Combine ground beef, salt, onion, bread crumbs, egg and tomato juice. Mix well. Press half of the mixture into bottom of well-buttered casserole. Top with the prepared stuffing mix. Cover with the remaining meat mixture and spread with a little melted butter. Bake at 350° for 1 hour. Heat soup and use as sauce. Makes about 8 servings.

When broiling hamburgers, chops or steaks, try adding a few drops of Worcestershire sauce to a small amount of melted butter and basting the meat several times.

PEPPER STEAK

- 2 lbs. round steak in ½" strips
- 3 T. oil
- 1 medium onion, diced
- ¼ c. soy sauce
- ¼ c. sugar
- 1 t. salt
- Pepper
- ¼ t. ginger
- 2 green peppers, cut in strips
- 4 tomatoes, quartered
- 1 T. cornstarch
- 1 c. bean sprouts (optional)

Brown strips of round steak in oil. Add onion, soy sauce, sugar, seasonings, green pepper, tomatoes, and ¼ cup of water. Cook for 15 minutes. Add 1 tablespoon of cornstarch with a little water; cook for 5 more minutes. Bean sprouts may be added last if desired. Serves 4 to 6.

HOT FERDINANDS

An easy and inexpensive meal, this recipe was concocted during the Depression. It was a favorite of my children, who named these tasty sandwiches after a popular story character of the time, Ferdinand the Bull.

- 1 lb. ground beef
- 1 small onion, grated
- ⅓ c. chili sauce
- ¾ t. salt
- ⅛ t. pepper
- 1 T. horseradish
- 6 hamburger buns

Mix ground beef, onion, chili sauce, horseradish and seasonings. Blend very well and spread on halves of buttered hamburger buns. Broil for seven minutes.

HAM PATTIES

- 1 lb. ground boiled ham
- 2 beaten eggs
- 2 T. minced parsley
- ½ c. fine bread crumbs
- ½ t. prepared mustard
- 2 c. crushed cornflakes
- 8 slices of canned pineapple with juice
- 8 maraschino cherries

Mix ground ham, eggs, parsley, bread crumbs and mustard. Form into 8 balls and roll in crushed corn flakes. Flatten each ball into a patty. Cut each pineapple slice in half, forming 2 thin rings. Place each patty between 2 slices of pineapple and place on buttered pan. Bake for ½ hour at 350°, basting with juice from canned pineapple. Place a cherry on top of each patty before serving.

HAM 'N' SWEETS

Use the same ingredients as above, omitting pineapple. Combine and form into 20 small balls. Combine 2 cups of mashed sweet potatoes, ½ cup brown sugar, ½ teaspoon salt and ¼ teaspoon cloves. Divide this mixture into 20 parts and enclose each ham ball in the sweet potato mixture. Roll in cornflakes and bake at 350° for 20 minutes. Serve with mushroom sauce.

Photo opposite: Pepper Steak

HAM ROLLUPS

- 8 slices white bread
- ¼ lb. boiled ham, ground
- 3 T. butter
- 1 egg
- ¼ c. chopped celery
- 2 T. minced parsley
- Seasonings
- 1 lb. boiled ham, cut into 8 slices
- 8 slices canned pineapple with juice

Soak slices of bread in water; squeeze dry. Add ground boiled ham, butter, egg, celery, parsley and seasonings. Divide this dressing among the 8 slices of ham. Roll each up, placing open edge down on a slice of pineapple. Place on buttered tin, baste with juice from canned pineapple and bake for 30 minutes at 350°. May be served with mushroom sauce.

Ham 'N' Eggers

HAM 'N' EGGERS

- 1 lb. baked or boiled ham, chopped
- 8 soda crackers
- 1 c. milk
- 8 eggs

Soak the soda crackers in milk, add chopped ham and mix as for meat loaf. Butter 8 muffin tins and pack sides and bottom with the ham mixture. Bake 20 minutes at 350°. Remove and drop an egg in each ham-lined muffin tin. Bake until egg is set.

HAM EN CROUTE

- 1 ham, 5-8 pounds
- ½ c. cherry preserves
- 2 T. corn syrup
- 4 c. biscuit mix
- 1 t. sage
- 2 T. prepared mustard
- ¾ c. shortening
- ⅔ c. milk
- 1 4½-oz. tin deviled ham
- 1 egg yolk
- Wine sauce

Bake ham for 2 hours at 325°. Combine cherry preserves with corn syrup and spoon over ham. Bake 10 more minutes at 350°, baste again and bake 15 minutes longer. Cool. Prepare biscuit dough 2 hours before serving. Combine biscuit mix, sage, prepared mustard, shortening and milk. Roll out to 12 x 22". Spread the deviled ham to 1½" from edges. Center the baked ham on the dough, fold over and seal pastry with a little water. Place sealed edge down on a buttered tin. Use scraps of dough and cut into small leaves with a sharp knife. Arrange these on top of ham and brush dough with egg wash made by mixing 1 egg yolk with 1 tablespoon of water. Bake at 350° for 1 hour or until golden brown. Allow to stand 10 minutes before slicing. Serve with wine sauce.

WINE SAUCE

Heat 2 cups of light or dark wine with the juice of 1 lemon. Add 2 tablespoons of cornstarch dissolved in 2 tablespoons of cold water; stir until slightly thickened. Serve warm.

CHICKEN CURRY

4 c. diced, cooked chicken
½ c. butter
6 T. flour
2 c. applesauce
1 envelope dry onion soup mix
2½ t. curry powder
½ t. ground ginger
¼ c. lemon juice

Melt butter. Add flour, applesauce, onion soup mix, curry powder, ginger and 2 cups water. Simmer for about ½ hour. Add lemon juice and chicken and heat thoroughly. Serve over cooked rice. Makes 4 to 6 servings.

ROAST VENISON

2½ c. dry red wine
½ c. apple cider
3 bay leaves
4 whole peppercorns
1 6-lb. venison roast
Salt
¼ c. butter
1 c. reserved marinade, strained

In shallow dish combine wine and apple cider. Add bay leaves and peppercorns. Marinate venison in mixture; cover and chill overnight, turning occasionally. Place meat fat side up on rack in roasting pan. Season with salt. Insert meat thermometer in center of thickest part of meat, not touching bone or resting in fat. Place in a 325° oven. Meanwhile, in 1-quart saucepan melt butter; add reserved marinade. Brush meat occasionally with marinade mixture. Roast to desired degree of doneness (about 25 minutes per pound for medium rare). Remove roast to warmed platter. Serve with Sour Cream Gravy.

SOUR CREAM GRAVY

1½ T. all-purpose flour
½ t. salt
¾ c. drippings from roast
½ c. dry red wine
1 c. dairy sour cream

In 1½-quart saucepan combine flour and salt; gradually add drippings, stir until smooth. Add wine. Stir over medium heat until thickened. Reduce heat to low, stir in sour cream. Heat to serving temperature.

HENS EN CROUTE

4 chicken breasts
½ c. prepared stuffing
3 c. flour
1½ c. shortening
1 t. salt
Ginger
1 egg yolk
Sauce Supreme

Prepare pastry of flour, shortening, salt, a pinch of ginger and about ¼ cup cold water. Roll out dough and cut into 8 circles. Bone and skin chicken breasts; cut in half lengthwise. Prepare your favorite stuffing and place about 1 tablespoon on each piece of chicken. Roll up and place each on a circle of dough. Encase the chicken breast in dough, place on a buttered tin and glaze with egg yolk mixed with water. Bake at 425° for 20 to 30 minutes. Serve with Sauce Supreme.

SAUCE SUPREME

Sauté 1 finely chopped onion in 6 tablespoons of butter. Add 4 tablespoons flour and 1 cup heavy cream. Season and add ½ cup wine; stir and heat thoroughly.

To give steak a new flavor, after broiling sprinkle with dry mustard and dot generously with butter. Place under the broiler just long enough to melt the butter.

BAKED FILLED CHICKEN BREASTS

4 chicken breasts
8 1-oz. slices of boiled ham or dried beef
8 slices of bacon
1 10½-oz. can cream of mushroom soup
1 c. sour cream

Skin and bone chicken breasts; cut each in half lengthwise. Place slice of boiled ham or dried beef on each. Roll up and wrap with a piece of bacon, securing with a toothpick. Place in deep, buttered pan and cover with cream of mushroom soup mixed with sour cream. Cover pan completely with foil and bake at 275° for 2½ hours. Uncover; bake an additional ½ hour. Serves 8.

PEACH-STUFFED CHICKEN BREASTS

6 chicken breasts
1 t. salt
3 fresh peaches
½ c. finely chopped onion
½ c. chopped cashews
½ t. powdered ginger
¼ c. butter
Fresh Peach Sauce

Bone and skin chicken breasts and cut in half lengthwise. Pound each to flatten and sprinkle with the salt. Make filling of peaches, peeled and cut into small pieces, onion, cashews and ginger. Place on each piece of chicken, roll up and secure with a toothpick. Melt butter in foil-lined tin and place stuffed chicken breasts in. Bake at 350° for 25 minutes, turn chicken and bake 20 minutes longer. Serve with sauce below.

Fresh Peach Sauce

Combine 2 fresh peaches, peeled and sliced, with ½ cup brown sugar, 2 teaspoons mustard, ¼ teaspoon salt, 1 cup sour cream and 1 tablespoon brandy. Heat for 5 minutes.

PARTY PERFECT CHICKEN

2 3-lb. chickens, cut up
6 T. flour
1½ t. salt
1 t. ginger
¾ c. butter
Curry Glaze (optional)

Shake pieces of chicken in a bag with the flour, salt and ginger. Melt the butter in a baking pan and roll chicken in butter, coating well. Arrange skin side up in a single layer and bake uncovered for 20 minutes at 400°. Turn chicken, brush with more butter and bake another 20 minutes, until nicely browned.

CHICKEN HAWAIIAN

6 coconuts
1¼ c. butter
3 c. flour
1 qt. milk
1½ t. salt
4 to 5 c. cooked, diced chicken
1 lb. fresh mushrooms, sliced
2 c. diced celery
1 small jar pimientos
2 c. flour
1 c. shortening
2 egg yolks

Saw coconuts in half. Scrape about 2 tablespoons of coconut meat from each half, grate and set aside. Prepare a cream sauce by stirring flour into 1 cup melted butter and adding milk. Add 1 teaspoon salt and cook, stirring, until thickened. Sauté the sliced mushrooms in ¼ cup butter. Combine grated coconut, cream sauce, mushrooms, celery, pimiento and diced chicken. Divide mixture and fill the twelve half shells. Make pastry by mixing 2 cups flour, 1 cup shortening, ½ teaspoon salt and 2-3 tablespoons of cold water or 7-Up. Roll out quite thin and cut into 15 circles to fit top of filled coconut shells. Crimp edges and make several slits in top for steam to escape. Brush tops with egg glaze made by beating two egg yolks with 2 tablespoons of water. Bake at 350° for one hour. Hint: Place shells on crumpled foil to bake and serve so they do not tip.

Curry Glaze

Dice 6 slices bacon; fry gently until brown. Add 1 medium apple, peeled and diced; 2 tablespoons flour, 1 tablespoon curry powder, 1 tablespoon sugar, 1 cup condensed beef broth, 2 tablespoons catsup and 2 tablespoons lemon juice. Heat together until boiling; stir until thickened. Brush chicken with the sauce and bake another 20 minutes. Serve with parsley-buttered rice.

Photo opposite:
Party Perfect Chicken with Curry Glaze

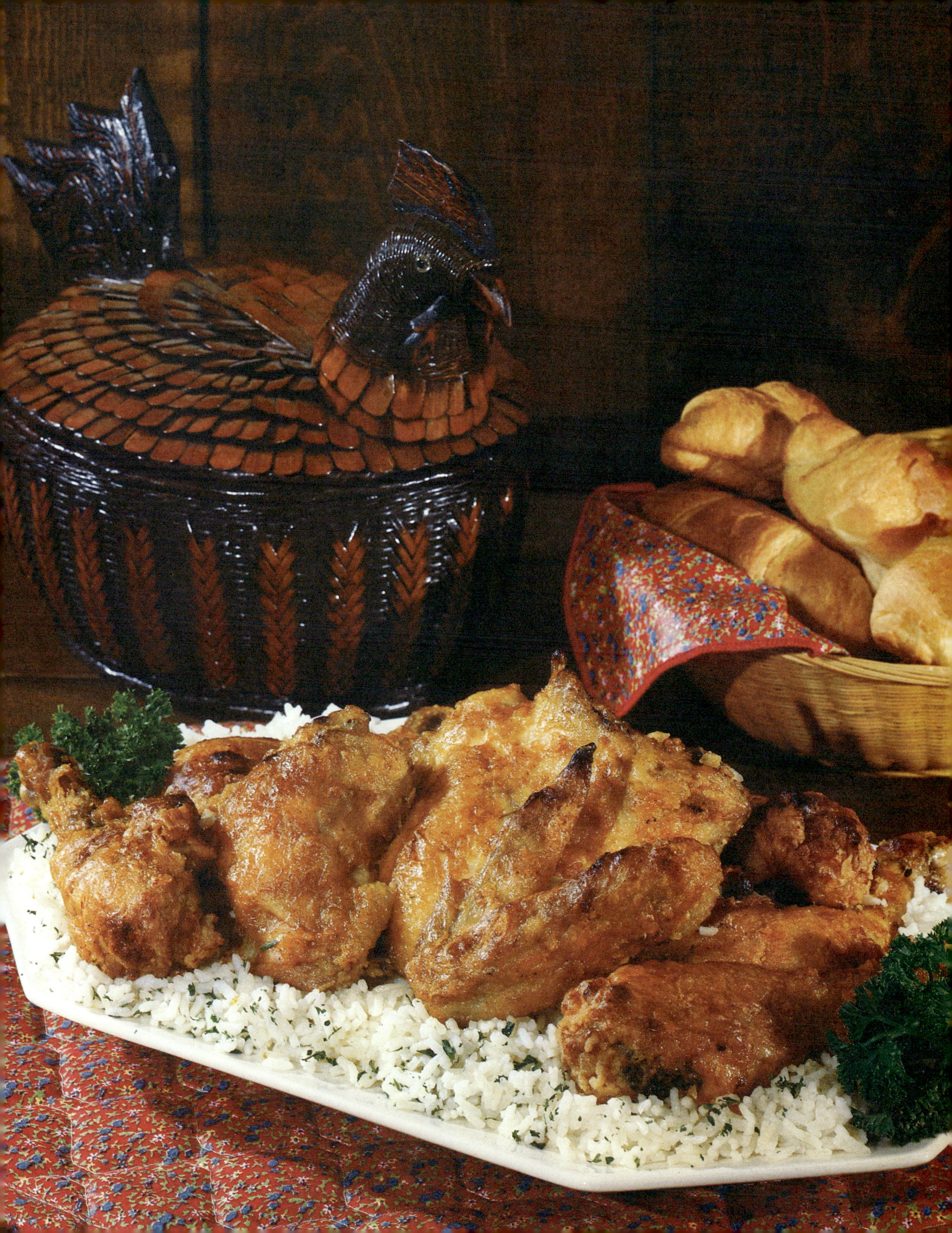

SEAFOOD

SHRIMP STROGANOFF

2 medium onions, chopped
3 T. butter
¼ c. diced celery
2 T. flour
4½ oz. tin of shrimp
½ pt. sour cream
¼ c. chopped chives

Sauté the onion in butter. Add celery and place in buttered casserole. Combine shrimp and flour; put on top of celery and onion. Combine sour cream and chives and spread over shrimp. Heat at 350° for 20 minutes. Serve on cooked rice. Serves 2-3.

SALMON PUDDING

1 1-lb. can salmon
1 c. milk
1 T. butter
½ t. salt
2 eggs, separated
2½ slices white bread, crusts removed
1 t. lemon juice
1 T. chili sauce

Bone and flake salmon. Heat milk, butter and salt; add egg yolks and bread, cut into small pieces. Remove from heat, add the lemon juice and chili sauce, and mix well with salmon. Last, fold in stiffly beaten egg whites. Place in casserole and bake for 30 minutes at 350°. Serves 4.

CRAB QUICHE

1 prepared pie crust
4½ oz. canned crab meat, flaked
2 T. chopped green onions
3 oz. cream cheese
2 T. dry vermouth
4 eggs
1 c. heavy cream
½ c. milk
½ t. salt
¼ t. crushed rosemary

Mix flaked crab meat with chopped onion, cream cheese and dry vermouth; spread in unbaked crust. Beat eggs with heavy cream, add milk and seasonings, and pour over crab mixture. Bake at 450° for 10 minutes. Reduce temperature to 350° and bake for 40 more minutes. Serve at once. Serves 6.

BAKED RED SNAPPER

3-4 lbs. red snapper
¾ c. diced celery
1 medium onion, diced
6 T. oil
1 qt. bread cubes
½ c. sour cream
½ t. salt
Paprika

Season the red snapper and fill loosely with the following stuffing: Sauté celery and onion in 4 tablespoons of oil. Add bread cubes and stir well; remove from heat. Add sour cream, salt and a little paprika. Place stuffed fish in baking pan, rubbing top of fish with rest of the oil. Bake at 350° for 40 to 60 minutes. Serves 6.

FLOUNDER ROLLUPS

2 10-oz. packages frozen broccoli spears
8 fillets of flounder
1 10½-oz. can cream of celery soup
½ c. mayonnaise
1 lemon

Cook broccoli spears; drain well. Divide spears among the fish fillets, place on center of fillet and roll up, securing with a toothpick. Put into a well-buttered pan or casserole. Mix undiluted cream of celery soup with the mayonnaise and the juice of the lemon. Pour mixture over flounder and bake at 350° for 20 minutes. Baste with sauce again and bake 15 to 20 minutes longer. Garnish with lemon slice twists. Slice lemon into ¼-inch slices and cut halfway through to the center of each slice; give a slight twist. Place on each serving with a bit of parsley.

SEAFOOD SOUFFLÉ

½ c. light cream
1 c. shredded sharp cheddar cheese
6 egg whites, stiffly beaten
1 c. flaked crab meat
½ t. salt
Pepper

Heat cream in double boiler. Add cheese and seasonings; remove from heat and cool slightly. Fold in the stiffly beaten egg whites, add crab meat, and place in a buttered casserole. Bake at 325° for 45 minutes; serve immediately.

Shrimp Creole

SHRIMP CREOLE

½ c. butter or margarine
4 medium onions, chopped
1 green pepper, chopped
2 c. diced celery
2 10½-oz. cans tomato soup
¼ t. sage
½ T. salt
½ c. brown sugar
2 lbs. cooked shrimp

Melt butter or margarine; add onions, green pepper and celery; sauté until tender but not brown. Add tomato soup plus 1 soup can of water, sage, salt and brown sugar. Simmer together for thirty minutes. Add shrimp and stir until shrimp are heated through. If mixture appears to be a bit thin, thicken by adding a little cornstarch mixed with water. Serves 8 generously. Serve on cooked rice.

SEAFOOD CASSEROLE

⅓ c. margarine
⅓ c. flour
2 t. prepared mustard
½ t. paprika
½ t. salt
2 t. brown sugar
1 T. grated onion
3 c. milk
6 oz. grated cheddar cheese
6½ oz. flaked crab meat
6 oz. tin lobster
1 lb. fresh cooked shrimp
Avocado garnish

Melt margarine, add flour and stir well. Add mustard, paprika, salt, sugar, onion and milk; cook until slightly thickened. Stir in grated cheese, remove from heat and mix with seafood. Place ingredients in large buttered casserole and bake for 25 minutes at 350°. The last 5 minutes, top casserole with slices of peeled avocado dipped in lemon juice. Radiate them from the center to resemble petals of a flower. Serves 10 to 12.

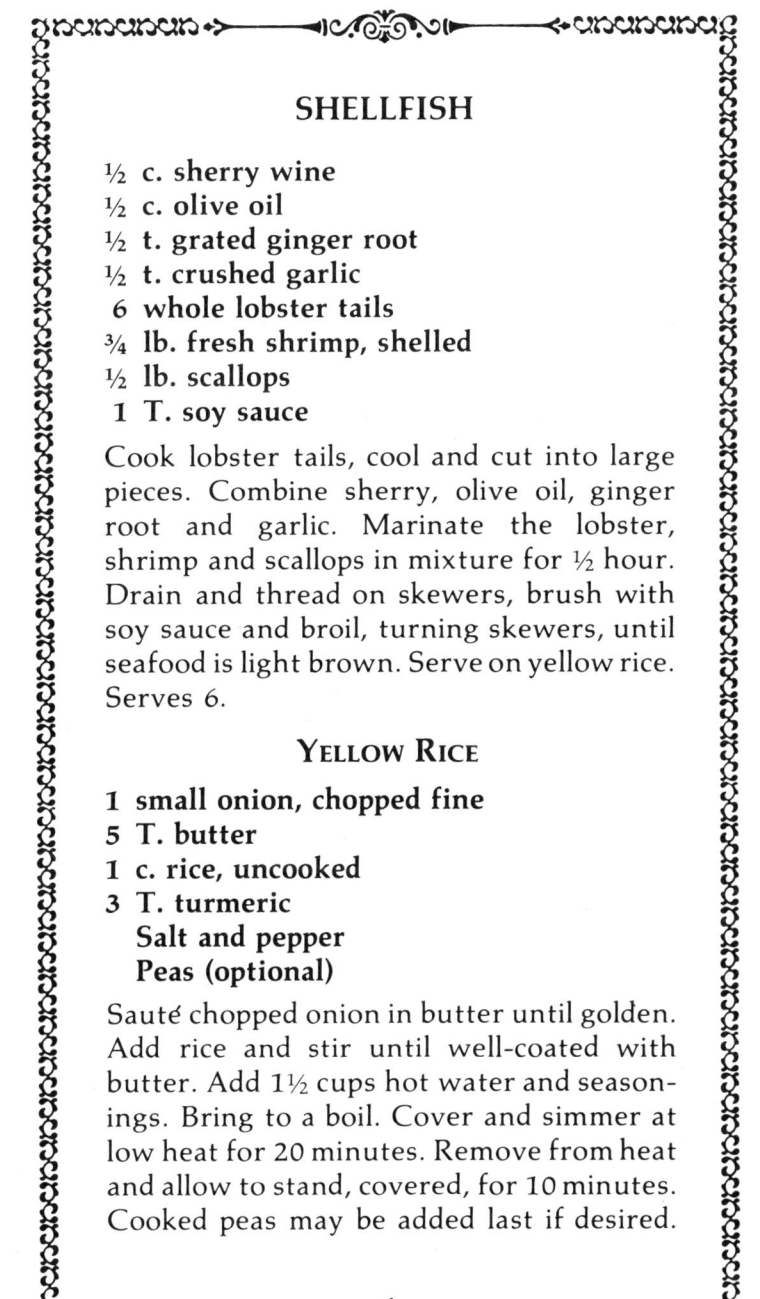

SHELLFISH

½ c. sherry wine
½ c. olive oil
½ t. grated ginger root
½ t. crushed garlic
6 whole lobster tails
¾ lb. fresh shrimp, shelled
½ lb. scallops
1 T. soy sauce

Cook lobster tails, cool and cut into large pieces. Combine sherry, olive oil, ginger root and garlic. Marinate the lobster, shrimp and scallops in mixture for ½ hour. Drain and thread on skewers, brush with soy sauce and broil, turning skewers, until seafood is light brown. Serve on yellow rice. Serves 6.

YELLOW RICE

1 small onion, chopped fine
5 T. butter
1 c. rice, uncooked
3 T. turmeric
Salt and pepper
Peas (optional)

Sauté chopped onion in butter until golden. Add rice and stir until well-coated with butter. Add 1½ cups hot water and seasonings. Bring to a boil. Cover and simmer at low heat for 20 minutes. Remove from heat and allow to stand, covered, for 10 minutes. Cooked peas may be added last if desired.

VEGETABLES

GREEN BEANS CAESAR

¾ c. bread cubes
3 T. oil
1 16-oz. can French-cut green beans
1 T. vinegar
1 T. sugar
1 t. chopped onion
  Salt
  Parmesan cheese

Sauté bread cubes in 2 tablespoons of oil until browned. Heat beans; drain. Heat vinegar, 1 tablespoon oil, sugar, chopped onion and a little salt; pour over beans. Top with the bread cubes and sprinkle with cheese. Serve immediately.

CRUNCHY TOMATOES

4 medium tomatoes
1 c. bread crumbs
2 T. brown sugar
2 T. butter
¼ t. garlic salt

Cut tomatoes in half. Mix bread crumbs, brown sugar, butter and garlic salt together like a streusel and sprinkle evenly over tomatoes. Bake at 350° for 10 minutes.

SPINACH SURPRISE

1 10-oz. pkg. frozen spinach
1 T. grated onion
2 T. lemon juice
1 t. salt
  Pepper
1 3-oz. pkg. cream cheese

Cook spinach; drain. Cube the cream cheese and gently add to the spinach with remaining ingredients. Serve at once with wedges of hard-boiled eggs sprinkled with paprika.

CARROT MOLD

4 c. grated fresh carrots
1½ t. salt
1 t. sugar
2 T. melted butter
½ c. fine bread crumbs
4 eggs, beaten
1 c. milk

Combine ingredients, mix well, and pour into a well-buttered ring mold or casserole. Steam in a pan of water in the oven at 325° for 1 hour. Good served with creamed peas.

> A teaspoon or two of lemon juice in the cooking water of white vegetables keeps them white.

BREADED CELERIAC WITH EGG SAUCE

1 large celery root
1 egg yolk, beaten
½ c. fine bread crumbs
¼ c. + 2 T. butter
1½ T. flour
½ c. beef bouillon
2 hard-boiled eggs, chopped
1 T. chives or green onion, chopped
1 t. dill weed
1 T. parsley

Peel celery root and slice into pieces ¼" thick. Cook until tender, saving the broth. Dip cooled slices of celery root into mixture of beaten egg yolk and bread crumbs. Brown carefully in ¼ cup butter. Serve with a sauce made with 2 tablespoons melted butter, flour, beef bouillon and ½ cup of the reserved broth. Season well and add the hard-boiled eggs, chives or onion, dill weed and parsley.

SPINACH EN CASSEROLE

1 10-oz. pkg. frozen spinach
1 T. butter
1 t. salt
　Pepper
¼ t. nutmeg
2 eggs, beaten
1 T. fine bread crumbs
4 slices bacon, diced

Heat the package of frozen spinach with the butter and seasonings. Combine the eggs and bread crumbs; add to above ingredients, and place in a buttered casserole. Top with diced bacon. You may also want to add about ¼ cup of sliced mushrooms, nuts, or chunks of cheddar cheese. Bake at 350° for 45 minutes. Serves 4.

SPINACH SOUFFLÉ

1 10-oz. pkg. chopped frozen spinach
5 T. butter
5 T. flour
1 t. salt
1½ c. milk
6 eggs, separated

Heat spinach to defrost; drain well and cool. Melt butter, add flour and salt, then slowly add the milk, cooking until slightly thickened. Add beaten egg yolks, stirring well to incorporate the eggs; add this mixture to the spinach. Beat egg whites until they form peaks; fold into spinach and place in casserole. Steam in pan of warm water at 300° for 1¼ hours. Serve immediately. Makes 6 servings.

CORN FRITTERS

2 c. whole kernel corn
1¾ c. flour
3 t. baking powder
½ t. salt
1 egg
1 c. milk
1 T. melted shortening
　Cooking oil

Mix corn with flour, baking powder and salt. Beat egg with milk; add to corn mixture. Combine with the shortening and then drop by teaspoonfuls into deep hot fat, frying 3 to 4 minutes. Drain on paper toweling and serve topped with powdered sugar and syrup. Makes about 18 fritters.

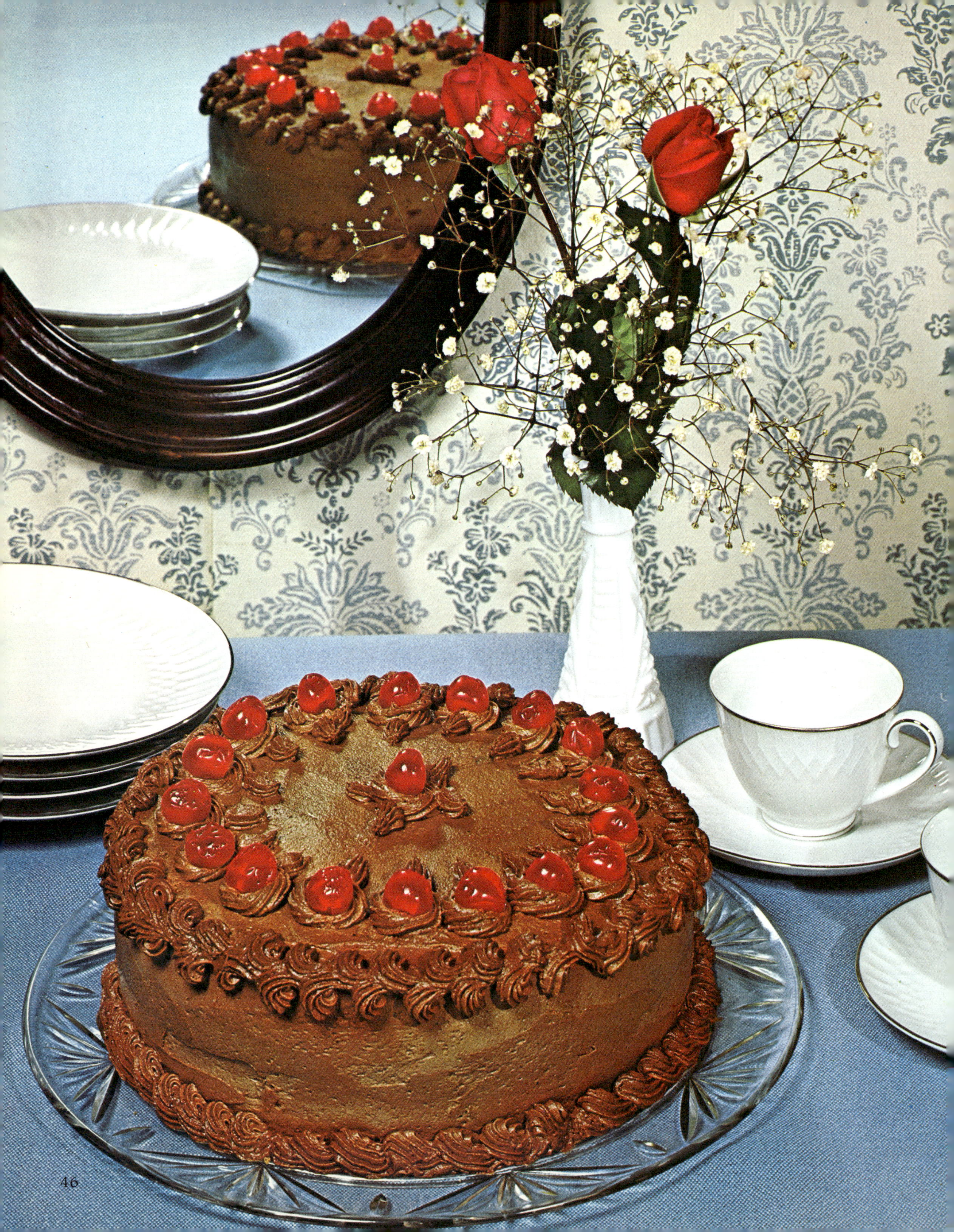

DESSERTS

KAPAZINA TORTE

A specialty of the house, this torte resembles the robes of Capuchin monks in Europe.

- 8 eggs, separated
- 1⅓ c. sugar
- 2½ t. baking powder
- 1 c. flour
- 1½ t. vanilla
- 3 squares semisweet chocolate, grated
- 1 c. finely ground nuts

Filling:
- 1 pt. heavy cream
- 12 maraschino cherries, quartered
- ¼ c. nuts, chopped
- 2 T. white rum or brandy

Easy Butter Creme Frosting

Beat egg yolks with sugar until sugar is dissolved. Add baking powder, flour, vanilla, grated chocolate and ground nuts. Fold in stiffly beaten egg whites. Pour batter into buttered springform and bake at 325° for 15 to 20 minutes. Cool and cut into 3 layers.

Filling: Whip cream until stiff; add maraschino cherry pieces, chopped nuts and rum or brandy. Spread filling between cake layers and cover with a chocolate butter creme frosting. Decorate with frosting swirls and cherries. Refrigerate or freeze torte.

COFFEE CREME TORTE

- 8 eggs, separated
- 1½ c. powdered sugar
- 2 t. baking powder
- ½ c. flour or finely ground nuts
- 3 T. instant powdered coffee
- 1 t. vanilla
- ¼ t. cream of tartar

Beat egg yolks very well. Add powdered sugar, baking powder, flour or ground nuts, instant coffee, and vanilla; mix thoroughly. Beat egg whites with cream of tartar until stiff peaks form; fold into batter. Bake in 3 well-buttered, floured 8" or 9" layer cake tins at 350° for 20 minutes. Cool. Carefully split each layer in half; fill and frost with any chocolate frosting. (Add 1 tablespoon powdered instant coffee to frosting for extra flavor.)

Easy Butter Creme Frosting

Cream 1 cup butter with 1 cup sugar. Add 1 teaspoon vanilla, ¾ cup flour, ⅔ cup milk and ½ cup cocoa; beat well.

THANKSGIVING TORTE

- 40 large marshmallows
- ¼ c. lemon juice
- 1¼ c. orange juice
- 2 T. unflavored gelatin
- 1 c. heavy cream, whipped
- Mandarin orange slices
- Ground nuts

Cook marshmallows, lemon juice, orange juice and 1¼ cup water in double boiler until marshmallows are softened. Dissolve gelatin in ¼ cup water and add to above mixture. Allow to cool and fold in whipped cream. Pour into 11" springform. Decorate top with mandarin orange slices and nuts; refrigerate.

Photo opposite: Kapazina Torte

ANGEL PIE

- 4 eggs, separated
- 1 t. cream of tartar
- 1½ c. sugar
- 1 lemon
- ½ c. heavy cream, whipped

Beat egg whites 15 minutes, until very stiff. Add cream of tartar when just fluffy. Slowly add 1 cup of sugar and beat for another 15 minutes. Place mixture in buttered pie tin. Bake 1 hour at 300°. Cool. In double boiler, beat egg yolks with ½ cup sugar. Add juice and grated rind of 1 lemon; stir and cook until thickened. Cool filling and pour over baked meringue. Top with whipped cream. Garnish with strawberries or other fruit if desired.

BLITZ TORTE

- 4 eggs, separated
- 1½ c. sugar
- ½ c. butter
- ¼ c. milk
- ½ c. flour
- 1 t. baking powder
- 2 t. vanilla
- ½ c. chopped nuts
- ½ c. heavy cream, whipped
- 1 pt. fresh sliced strawberries

Cream ½ cup sugar with the butter. Blend in beaten egg yolks, then add milk and flour alternately. Add baking powder and 1 teaspoon vanilla. Place mixture in 2 buttered 8-inch cake tins. In a separate bowl, beat egg whites until stiff, add 1 cup sugar and continue beating while adding 1 teaspoon vanilla and the chopped nuts. Spread half of this meringue over each layer in cake tins. Bake at 375° for 25 minutes. When cool, spread 1 layer with half of the strawberries and whipped cream; place second layer on top and top with remaining strawberries and cream.

PEACH IMPERIAL

- 3 fresh peaches
- ¼ c. butter
- 1 c. flour
- ½ t. salt
- ¼ t. baking powder
- ⅓ c. shortening
- 1 egg yolk
- Brandy Sauce

Wash and dry fresh peaches. Cream butter and spread over each peach. Mix flour, salt, baking powder, shortening and 1½ tablespoons hot water as pie crust. Chill mixture well and roll dough out quite thin. Cut into strips 1" x 10". Encircle each peach with the pastry and brush with an egg glaze made by beating 1 egg yolk with 1 teaspoon water. Bake at 375° for 40 minutes. Serve hot with the following sauce.

Brandy Sauce

Cream ¼ cup butter with 1 cup powdered sugar; add 1 egg white (unbeaten) and 2 tablespoons of brandy, last.

FROZEN LEMON DESSERT

- 3 eggs, separated
- 1¼ c. sugar
- 1½ lemons
- 2 c. crushed vanilla wafers
- ½ c. heavy cream, whipped

Beat egg yolks with ¾ cup sugar and the juice and grated rind of 1½ lemons. Cook until transparent in double boiler; cool. Beat egg whites until stiff, add ½ cup sugar, and fold into cooled cooked mixture. Fold in the whipped cream. Line an ice-cube tray with buttered foil. Cover bottom with vanilla wafer crumbs, reserving some for the top. Pour in lemon mixture and top with remaining cookie crumbs and a few nuts if desired. Freeze. To serve, simply lift out dessert in the foil and slice.

COCONUT MACAROON DESSERT

- 12 large coconut macaroon cookies, crushed
- 1 c. heavy cream, whipped
- 1 pt. raspberry sherbet
- 1 pt. lime sherbet

Place ½ the cookie crumbs in bottom of a foil-lined bread pan. Top with a layer of whipped cream. Add spoonfuls of lime and raspberry sherbet alternately. Top with remaining whipped cream and cookie crumbs. Freeze. To serve, lift dessert in foil and slice. Serves 8.

CHERRY CAKE QUICKIE

- ½ c. + 1 t. butter
- 1 egg
- ½ c. milk
- 1¼ c. flour
- 1 t. baking powder
- ¼ t. salt
- 1 c. drained sour cherries

Mix all ingredients except cherries; beat well. Place in buttered cake pan and top with cherries. Bake at 350° for 25 minutes. Spread with a thin icing while cake is still warm. Refrigerate until set.

STRAWBERRY MACAROON WHIP

- 2 c. coarse macaroon cookie crumbs
- 1 pt. fresh strawberries, sliced
- ¼ c. sugar
- 3 T. port or muscatel
- 1 c. heavy cream, whipped

Sprinkle sugar over strawberries. Fold all ingredients together gently and pile into parfait or sherbet glasses. Top with additional whipped cream and a strawberry or cherry. Refrigerate until serving time.

EASY CHERRIES JUBILEE

1 #2 can dark cherries (21 oz.)
1 T. cornstarch
¼ t. salt
½ t. cinnamon
2 c. brandy

Heat juice from canned cherries with cornstarch, salt and cinnamon; cook until slightly thickened. Add 36 pitted cherries. Place in chafing dish and add 2 cups warm brandy. Light and stir while *en flambe*. Serve flaming over 3 or 4 servings of ice cream.

To flame a fruitcake or dessert, dip several cubes of sugar in a small amount of lemon extract, then place on dessert. Light immediately—a lovely blue flame!

HEAVENLY PUMPKIN PIE

1 c. flour
½ c. butter
1 egg yolk
¾ t. salt
¼ c. powdered sugar
1 3½ oz. pkg. vanilla pudding
½ c. brown sugar
½ t. cinnamon
¼ t. nutmeg
¼ t. ginger
1¼ c. evaporated milk
1 T. butter, melted
1¾ c. canned pumpkin

Mix flour with butter, egg yolk, ½ teaspoon salt and the powdered sugar. Pat into pie tin, but do not bake. Mix the vanilla pudding mix with brown sugar, cinnamon, nutmeg, ginger, and ¼ teaspoon salt. Add evaporated milk, melted butter and the pumpkin. Pour mixture into pie shell and bake at 375° for 15 minutes. Reduce heat to 350° and bake an additional 30 minutes.

DANISH RUM PUDDING

2 T. unflavored gelatin
6 eggs, separated
½ c. sugar
2 c. scalded milk
½ c. light cream
6 T. rum
Raspberry sauce

Dissolve gelatin in ½ cup water and allow to stand 5 minutes. Beat the egg yolks well with sugar; add scalded milk and cream. Pour above mixture into double boiler and cook, stirring continuously until mixture coats the spoon. Remove and add the dissolved gelatin; chill until mixture begins to thicken. Blend in rum; beat egg white until stiff and gently fold into first mixture. Rinse a ring mold or other fancy mold with cold water. Turn in the pudding and chill until firm. Serve with Raspberry Sauce.

RASPBERRY SAUCE

Force a 12-oz. package of frozen raspberries (defrosted) through a sieve. Blend in ½ cup sugar and ½ cup water. Add 1½ teaspoons cornstarch mixed with 1 tablespoon water. Stir gently and boil for 3 minutes. Cool and refrigerate until needed.

PUMPKIN MALLOW PIE

½ lb. marshmallows
1 c. canned pumpkin
¼ t. salt
1 t. cinnamon
¼ t. ground cloves
1 c. heavy cream

Place marshmallows, canned pumpkin, salt, cinnamon and ground cloves in double boiler. Heat until marshmallows are melted, then cool for 1 hour. Fold in stiffly beaten cream. Pour mixture into a baked pie shell. Chill for 2 hours. Serve with swirl of whipped cream to which a small amount of candied ginger has been added. May also be topped with a small cheese pumpkin.

Photo opposite:
Easy Cherries Jubilee

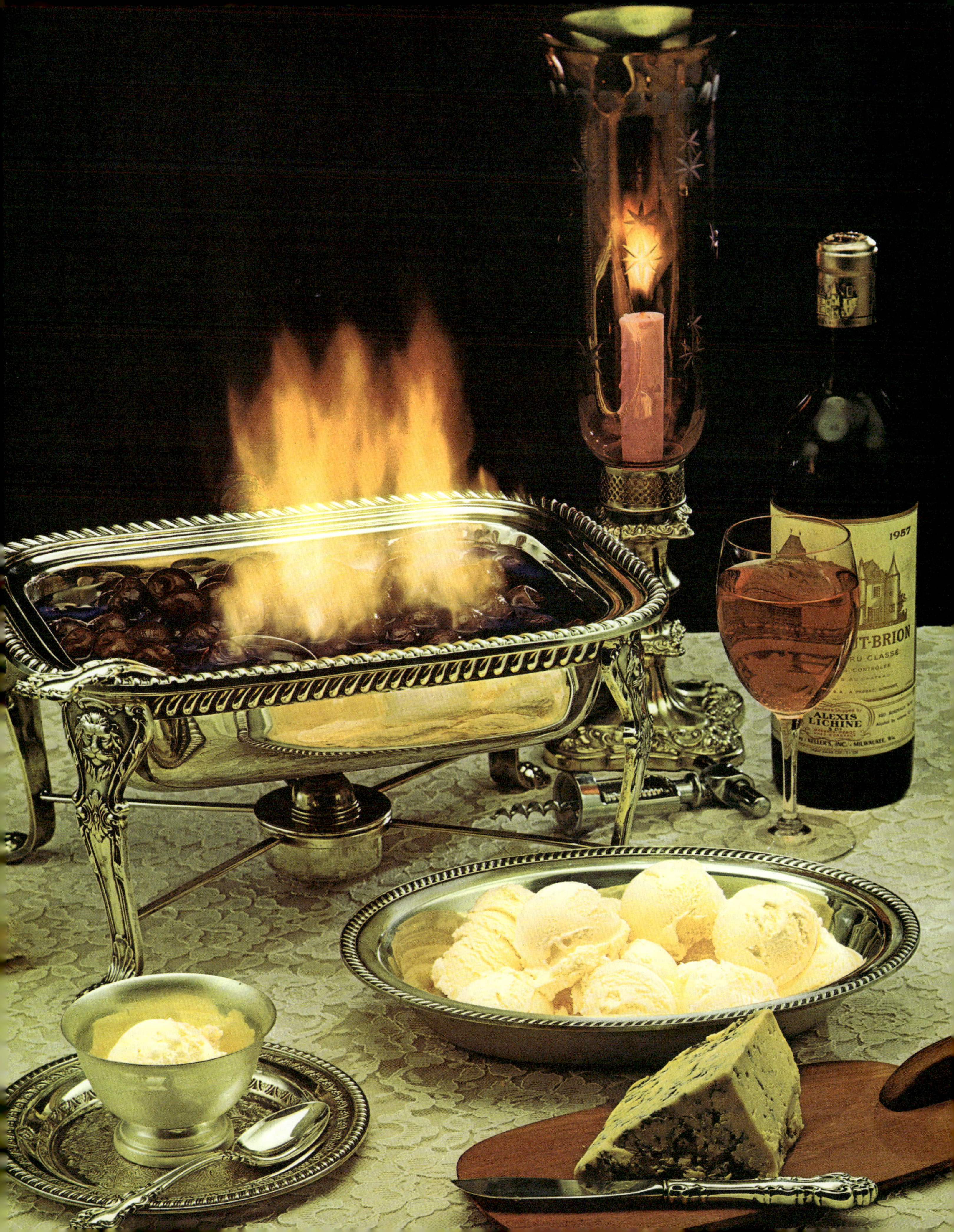
1957
ALEXIS
LICHINE

APPLE-NUT DESSERT

- 3 medium apples
- 1 egg
- ½ c. sugar
- ¼ c. flour
- ½ t. salt
- 2 t. baking powder
- 1 t. vanilla
- ¼ c. chopped nuts
- Whipped cream

Beat egg with sugar. Add flour, salt, baking powder and vanilla and mix well. Pour half of the batter into a well-buttered 6-x8-inch tin. Peel, core and dice apples and arrange on top of batter. Top with remainder of batter and spread as well as possible. (Batter will spread as it bakes.) Sprinkle nuts on top and bake at 350° for 25 minutes. Cut into squares and top each with a dab of whipped cream.

BOURBON POUND CAKE

- 1 lb. butter
- 3 c. sugar
- 8 eggs, separated
- 3 c. flour
- ⅔ c. bourbon
- 2 t. vanilla
- 2 t. almond extract
- ½ c. chopped nuts

Cream butter with 2 cups sugar. Add egg yolks one at a time, beating well after each addition. Add flour alternately with the combined bourbon, vanilla and almond extract. Beat egg whites with 1 cup sugar until stiff but not dry. Fold mixtures together. Sprinkle ½ cup of chopped nuts in bottom of well-buttered tube pan, then carefully turn in batter. Bake at 350° for 1½ hours. Slice into thin pieces to serve.

Orange Cake

DATE CAKE

1½ c. dates, pitted
½ t. baking soda
2 T. butter
½ c. sugar
½ c. brown sugar
1 c. flour
½ t. salt
1 egg
1 t. instant coffee
1 c. chopped nuts
Cream Cheese Frosting

Cut up dates and put in saucepan with baking soda and 1¼ cups water. Cook for 10 minutes and cool. Cream butter with sugar, flour, salt, egg, date mixture, and instant coffee dissolved in ¼ cup water. Mix well with the chopped nuts and pour into a well-buttered tube pan. Bake at 350° for 1 hour.

CREAM CHEESE FROSTING

Cream a 3-oz. package of cream cheese with 1 tablespoon milk. Add 1½ cups powdered sugar and 1 teaspoon vanilla and stir until smooth.

ICED ZABAGLIONE

6 egg yolks
¼ c. sugar
½ c. Marsala wine
1 envelope unflavored gelatin
1 c. heavy cream, whipped
1 t. vanilla

Combine egg yolks and sugar in double boiler over medium heat. Beat until sugar is dissolved; mixture will be light and creamy. Add wine and continue cooking for 6 minutes, until soft peaks form. Remove and cool. Add gelatin dissolved in 3 tablespoons of hot water and cool. Last, fold in whipped cream and vanilla. Serve in parfait glasses. Garnish with shaved chocolate. Serves 6.

ORANGE CAKE

8 eggs, separated
1⅓ c. sugar
½ t. salt
1 c. flour
Rind of 1 orange
¼ c. orange juice

Beat egg yolks with ⅔ cup sugar and salt. Combine flour and orange rind; add to egg yolk mixture alternately with the orange juice. Beat the egg whites with remaining sugar and fold gently into first mixture. Baked in ungreased angel food cake tin for 1 hour at 325°.

CRYSTALLIZED ROSE PETALS

Separate petals, removing apex. Gently wash petals and dry with paper toweling. Spread out on a cookie sheet and allow to dry overnight. Mix an egg white with 1 tablespoon of water and beat with a fork until fluffy. Brush 1 side of each petal with the mixture, lay on foil and sprinkle with granulated sugar. Dry overnight at room temperature. Repeat for other side of petals. Store petals in a glass jar and use them to garnish cakes, etc.

GRAHAM LOG

½ lb. graham cracker crumbs
½ lb. large marshmallows
12 maraschino cherries
1 lb. dates, cut fine
5 oz. can evaporated milk

Mix ingredients together and shape into a log with fingers. Sprinkle with more graham crumbs and refrigerate. To serve, slice and top with whipped cream. 10-12 servings.

CREAM CHEESE TORTE

Graham Cracker Crust
- 16 oz. cream cheese
- ½ c. sugar
- 5 eggs, separated
- 2 c. sour cream
- 1 T. lemon juice
- 2 t. vanilla

Line a 9" buttered springform with crumb pastry. Cream together cream cheese, sugar, egg yolks, sour cream, lemon juice and vanilla. Last, gently fold in five stiffly beaten egg whites. Pour mixture into crumb-lined tin. Bake at 300° for 1 hour. Turn off heat and allow cake to remain in oven for ½ hour with oven door closed. This prevents shrinking. When cool, chill in refrigerator. Serve with berries and whipped cream.

Graham Cracker Crust

Combine 2 cups of graham cracker crumbs and ½ cup melted butter with 1½ teaspoons cinnamon and ½ cup sugar.

CHEESELESS CHEESE TORTE

Graham Cracker Crust
- 4 eggs, separated
- 14 oz. sweetened condensed milk
- ⅓ c. lemon juice
- 1 t. grated lemon rind
- 1 t. vanilla

Line a springform pan with the graham cracker crust and bake 10 minutes. Beat egg yolks; add condensed milk, lemon juice, lemon rind and vanilla. Last, fold in stiffly beaten egg whites. Pour mixture over baked crust, sprinkle with crumbs and bake at 325° for 30 minutes. Leave in oven with door closed for 1 hour after baking. Serve with whipped cream.

Strawberry Glaze for Cheese Torte
- 1 qt. fresh strawberries
- ¾ c. sugar
- ¼ t. salt
- 1½ T. cornstarch
- 1 t. butter

Crush 1 cup of the strawberries. Add sugar, salt, cornstarch and ¼ cup cold water. Boil for 2 minutes. Add butter and a little red food coloring. Arrange whole berries on top of torte, spread over the cooled glaze and chill.

SCHAUM TORTE, UNBAKED

- 6 egg whites
- 2 c. sugar
- 1 t. baking powder
- 1 T. vinegar
- 1 t. vanilla

Heat oven to 500°. Beat egg whites for a full 15 minutes. Add sugar and continue beating for another 15 minutes. Add remaining ingredients. Pour mixture into buttered springform and place in oven. Turn off heat. Leave in oven for at least 6 hours or overnight. DO NOT OPEN OVEN. Top with berries and whipped cream.

UNBAKED CHEESECAKE

Graham Cracker Crust
- 1 8-oz. pkg. cream cheese
- ¼ c. confectioners' sugar
- 1 t. vanilla
- 1 c. heavy cream, whipped
- 1 #2 can blueberry or strawberry pie filling

Pat graham cracker crust into large pie tin. Cream together cream cheese, confectioners' sugar and vanilla. Fold in the whipped cream and place on crust; refrigerate several hours. Top with pie filling and sprinkle a few graham cracker crumbs over the top. You may serve small portions as this is very rich.

Photo opposite:
Unbaked Cheesecake

THE WAY TO
A FRIEND'S HOUSE

IS NEVER LONG

MERINGUES, QUICK AND EASY

4 egg whites
¼ t. cream of tartar
1½ c. sugar
1 t. almond or vanilla extract
Filling

Beat egg whites with cream of tartar for 15 minutes. Gradually add sugar and continue beating for another 15 minutes. Add almond or vanilla extract. Place meringue mixture on a greased cookie sheet which has been covered with buttered waxed paper. Drop by large tablespoonfuls or squeeze in circles through a pastry tube, allowing space between each mound. Bake 10 minutes at 300°. Turn off heat and allow meringues to remain in oven 5 minutes longer. Top with strawberries and whipped cream or fill depression in center with chocolate Filling Supreme.

CHOCOLATE FILLING SUPREME

Beat 2 egg whites with ½ cup sugar and 2 tablespoons cocoa until smooth in double boiler, over hot but not boiling water. Still beating constantly, add ¾ cup butter. ½ teaspoon essence of peppermint can also be added to filling. Cool and fill meringues; top with a swirl of whipped cream.

PEACH LADYFINGER DESSERT

½ c. butter
1 c. powdered sugar
2 eggs, separated
½ t. almond extract
1 16-oz. can sliced peaches
20 ladyfingers

Cream butter and powdered sugar. Add egg yolks, almond extract, and beaten egg whites. Place 10 ladyfingers, split in half, in bottom of bread tin. Top with half of the filling and half of the drained peaches. Place remainder of ladyfingers, split in half, on the filling; top with remainder of filling and peach slices. Refrigerate. Serve with whipped cream if desired.

BAKED ALASKA EN FLAMBÉ

1 angel food cake
1 16-oz. pkg. frozen strawberries
1 qt. vanilla ice cream
5 egg whites
⅔ c. sugar

Scoop out the center of an angel food cake, leaving sides, bottom, and center around the tube intact. Fill with unthawed strawberries and top with ice cream. Place cake on a wooden board about 1 inch larger than cake and covered with aluminum foil. Beat egg whites until very stiff. Add sugar, beating until sugar is dissolved. Spread over the entire cake, sealing well. Set oven at 450° then turn down to 400° to bake meringue for 12 minutes. Remove and serve immediately or freeze; do not defrost before using. Dip several sugar cubes in lemon extract or brandy, place on top of baked meringue and ignite.

COFFEE LOG CAKE

¾ c. flour
1 t. baking powder
¼ t. salt
4 eggs, separated
¾ c. sugar
1 t. vanilla
½ c. heavy cream, whipped
2 T. sugar
2 t. instant coffee

Mix flour, baking powder and salt. Beat egg yolks with ¾ cup sugar and vanilla; add flour mixture. Beat egg whites until stiff and fold in first mixture. Line a long jelly roll tin with buttered wax paper and pour in batter. Bake at 350° for 15 minutes; cool. Remove and place cake on a towel which has been sprinkled with powdered sugar. Combine whipped cream, remaining sugar and the instant coffee and spread this filling over the cake. Roll cake lengthwise and refrigerate. Frost with a butter frosting. Serves 8.

COUPE MAXIMS

6 fresh peaches
¼ c. sugar
¼ c. kirsch
1½ pt. pistachio ice cream
Raspberry Sauce

Peel and stone peaches; sprinkle with sugar. Cover with kirsch and allow to stand 30 minutes. Arrange 3 peach halves in each individual compote. Cover each with 2 scoops of ice cream. Spoon Raspberry Sauce over and serve.

Raspberry Sauce

Crush 1 pint of fresh raspberries. Add ¼ cup sugar and 3 tablespoons water; bring mixture to a boil. Add 1 teaspoon cornstarch mixed with 1 teaspoon water; cook for a few minutes. Strain and chill before serving over compote.

CHOCOLATE ROLL

5 eggs, separated
1 c. powdered sugar
3 T. cocoa
1 T. cornstarch
1 t. vanilla
1 c. heavy cream, whipped
Chocolate Sauce

Beat egg yolks with the powdered sugar, cocoa, cornstarch, and vanilla. Fold in 5 stiffly beaten egg whites. Spread mixture in greased jelly roll pan and bake at 350° for 8 minutes. Place on sugared wax paper or towel. Roll up and cool. Unroll and fill with whipped cream; roll up again.

Chocolate Sauce

Cook 1 tablespoon cocoa, 1 cup sugar, 4 tablespoons flour, 1 cup hot water, 1 teaspoon vanilla and ½ teaspoon salt until very thick.

Chocolate Roll

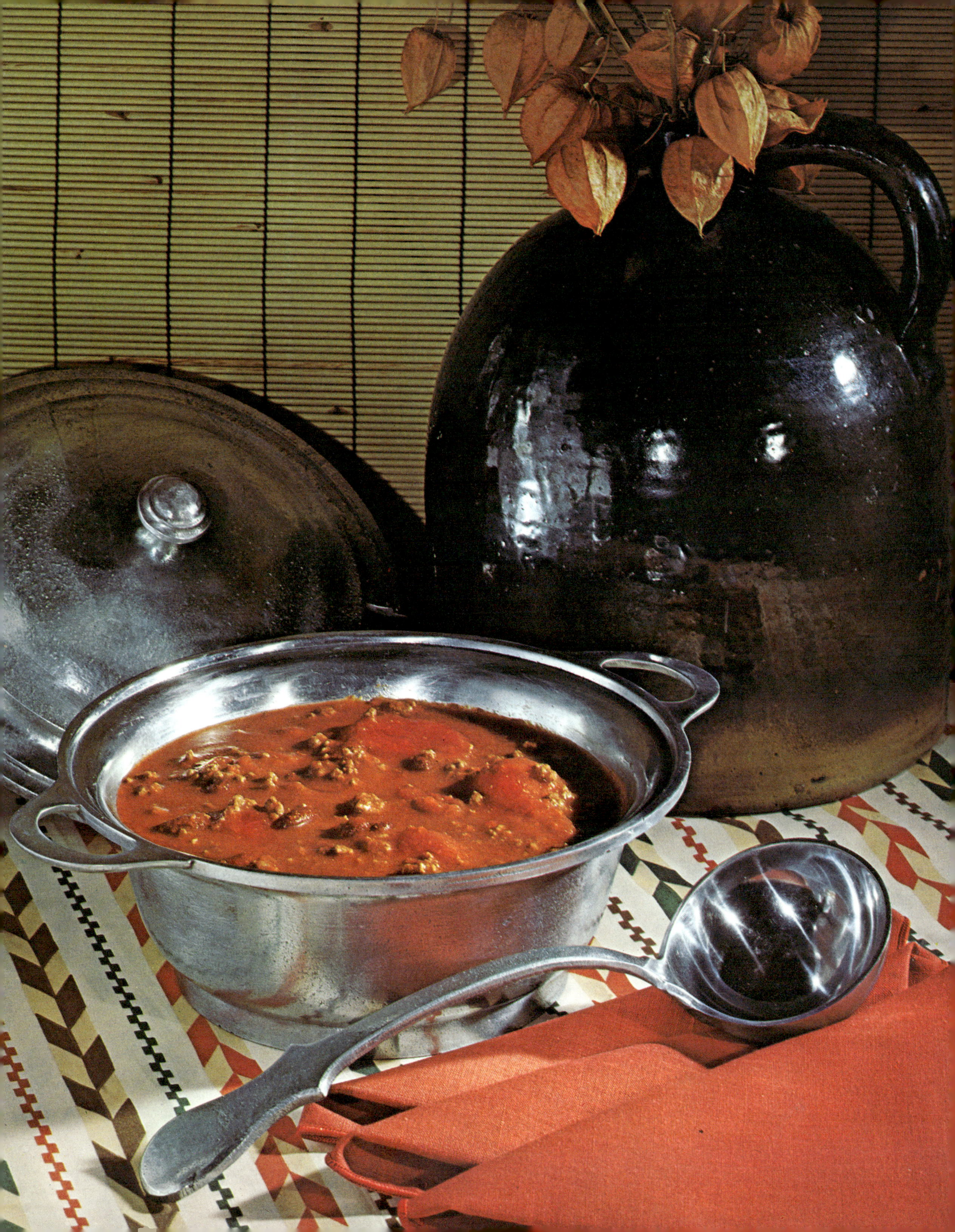

COOKING FOR A CROWD

CHILI

- 6 lbs. ground beef
- 20 large onions
- 2 large bunches celery
- 4 T. salt
- ¼ c. oil
- 6 10½-oz. cans tomato soup
- 3 15-oz. cans kidney beans
- Chili powder to taste

Sauté beef in oil until slightly browned. Add diced onions and celery and sauté for about 5 minutes. Drain. Add tomato soup, salt and chili powder; cook for 15 minutes. Add drained kidney beans and heat for 5 minutes. Serves 25 guests.

ALMOND-CHICKEN CASSEROLE

- 2 1-lb. loaves of bread
- 1 large bunch of celery
- 2 large onions
- 3 T. bacon drippings or shortening
- 1 T. sage
- 2 eggs
- 5 to 6 c. diced cooked chicken
- 2 10½-oz. cans cream of mushroom soup
- 1 13-oz. can evaporated milk
- ½ c. slivered almonds
- Salt
- Pepper

Break bread into crumbs. Dice the celery and slice onions fine, then cook both in 1½ pints water until tender. Drain and save the broth; add broth to bread crumbs. To this mixture add bacon drippings, sage, eggs, and salt and pepper to taste. Butter a large casserole and press dressing on bottom and sides, reserving one cup or more for the top. Add the diced chicken. Pour soup and evaporated milk, both undiluted, over the casserole. Top with reserved dressing and the slivered almonds. Bake for 1 hour at 350°. Serves 16 to 20 guests.

CRANBERRY RELISH

- 1 lb. cranberries
- 2 c. sugar
- 1 orange
- 2 apples, cored

Grind cranberries in blender or food grinder. Finely chop the unpeeled orange and apples. Mix all ingredients and refrigerate overnight. Serves over 20 guests at 2 to 3 tablespoons per serving.

OVEN-BAKED RICE

Mix 1 cup of beef consommé with 1 cup water. Add 1 cup long grain uncooked rice, 1 teaspoon salt and ¼ cup margarine. Cover and bake at 350° for 45 minutes. Tastes like wild rice and serves 10-12 guests.

EASY BAKED CHICKEN

Divide chicken into number of serving pieces needed and place each on a piece of foil. Top each piece with 1 teaspoon of butter, 1 teaspoon dry onion soup mix and 1 tablespoon light cream. Wrap loosely and bake 1 hour at 350°.

CALIFORNIA CHICKEN SALAD

- 4 lbs. cooked diced chicken
- 2 lbs. seeded Tokay or green grapes, halved
- 1 large bunch celery
- 1½ c. coarsely chopped nutmeats
- 3 c. sliced cooked mushrooms
- ¼ to ½ c. mayonnaise

Cut celery diagonally into small pieces. Combine with remaining ingredients and serve on lettuce or other greens. Makes 25 servings.

Photograph opposite: Chili

GERMAN POTATO SALAD

- 8 lbs. potatoes
- 1 lb. bacon, diced
- 3 T. flour
- ½ c. sugar
- 1½ T. salt
- ½ c. vinegar
- 1 medium onion, diced

Cook potatoes in jackets until tender; cool and peel. Dice bacon and fry over low heat until crisp. Drain, retaining fat, and dry bacon on paper toweling. Mix flour with ¼ cup bacon fat, add sugar and salt and stir well over low heat. Slowly add vinegar and 2¼ cups water. Cook, stirring until mixture starts to thicken; add onion. Slice the potatoes; combine with sauce and ½ of the crisp bacon. Sprinkle remainder of bacon on top. Minced parsley may also be added. Serves 20 to 25.

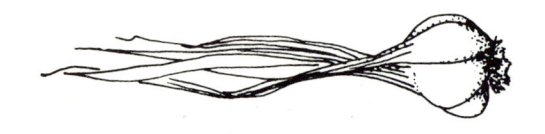

SPAGHETTI

- 2 lbs. spaghetti
- 4 lbs. ground beef
- 2 large onions, chopped
- ¼ c. oil
- 1 8-oz. can mushroom pieces, drained
- 2 green peppers, chopped
- 2 T. salt
- 2 T. sugar
- 6 10½-oz. cans tomato soup
- 1½ lbs. cheddar cheese, grated

Cook spaghetti until almost tender; drain. Brown meat and onions in oil for about 10 minutes. Add mushrooms, green pepper, salt, sugar and 4 cans of soup. Mix well with the drained spaghetti and top with remaining soup and the grated cheese. Place mixture in a large casserole and keep in low-temperature oven until ready to serve. Serves 25.

MINT MALLOW SALAD

- 1 3-oz. pkg. lime gelatin
- 1 10½-oz. bag miniature marshmallows
- 1 21-oz. can crushed pineapple
- 1 8-oz. box butter mints
- 2 1½-oz. envelopes Dream Whip

Dissolve gelatin in 1 cup boiling water; add marshmallows. Stir well until gelatin and marshmallows dissolve. Add pineapple and juice. Refrigerate for two hours, stirring often while mixture starts to congeal. Prepare Dream Whip according to directions. Crush the mints with a rolling pin; fold mints and Dream Whip into gelatin mixture. Pour into 9- x 13-inch pan and freeze overnight. Serves 20 to 24.

HAM LOAF

- 3 lbs. cooked ham, ground
- 2½ c. bread crumbs
- 1 large onion, diced
- 4 eggs, beaten
- 2 c. milk
- 2¼ c. tomato soup, undiluted
- Pepper

Mix the ground ham, bread crumbs, onion, eggs, and pepper with milk. Place mixture in large casserole and pour the undiluted soup over the top. Bake at 325° for 1½ to 2 hours. Serves 25.

FONDUE

- 3 lbs. Swiss cheese, grated
- 9 T. flour
- 1½ t. salt
- ½ t. pepper
- ½ t. nutmeg
- 6 c. milk, buttermilk or beer
- ½ c. white wine
- ½ t. garlic salt

Sprinkle flour over the grated cheese; add remaining ingredients except wine. Cook until thickened; add wine and stir. Serve from chafing dish with pieces of French bread. Serves 25 guests.

A FEW HINTS FOR ENTERTAINING

I have found that the most important thing to remember when preparing food is that eating involves seeing as well as tasting. Use simple garnishes for food, those which are eye-appealing and edible. If food coloring is used, keep the colors light and delicate. Use your own ingenuity when designing a centerpiece. Flowers from the garden or even weeds can be arranged in a quaint old teapot. If flowers aren't available, fresh fruits can make an attractive centerpiece, arranged in a nice bowl or woven basket.

An easy way to serve a large number of guests is with a buffet. A few simple preparations will help things run smoothly. First of all, use a large table when possible. The food won't look as crowded and your guests will have more room in which to serve themselves. If you can, form a line on either side of the table. It is also nice to have an assistant to serve the hot entrée; it is sometimes messy when people help themselves.

Another way to keep the food looking nice is to provide small plates that can be replenished often. In this way, the buffet still looks nice for the last guests. It is also a good idea to serve individual butter pats.

To keep food in a buffet warm, you may use chafing dishes with canned heat, electric units or alcohol burners. It is best to put the hot foods at the end of the buffet to be served last. The plates, too, can be warmed, either by using a plate warmer or by rinsing them in hot water.

Use cold plates and bowls to keep salads or other foods cold. These foods should be kept well-iced until serving. Trays of seafood or gelatin molds may be set over trays filled with ice cubes.

It is not necessary to buy expensive foods to make a party successful, but prepare recipes that are tried and true. Experiment ahead of time, not on the day of the party. Make out your guest list, menu and a shopping list in advance, so that food and arrangements can be made at a leisurely pace. In this way, you will remain a friendly, relaxed hostess and your party is sure to be more enjoyable for both you and your guests.

INDEX

APPETIZERS
Baked Toast, 12
Brandied Cheese Spread, 3
Cheese Overs in Miniature, 4
Cheese Puffs, 12
Cheese Straws, 5
Cheesies, 8
Cocktail Prunes, 5
Coconut Curry Balls, 12
Crab Snacks, 6
Cream Cheese Pastry, 5
Creamy Tomato Cocktail, 11
Deviled Ham Puffs, 8
Hen on the Nest, 6
Hors d'Oeuvres Pie, 4
Hot Crab Spread, 3
Individual Pizzas, 6
Liver Paste, 8
Orange Sugared Walnuts, 12
Party Pink Champagne Punch, 11
Paté 'N' Miniature, 8
Pineapple Fizz, 11
Quiche Lorraine, 5
Raspberry Cocktail, 11
Sauerbraten Meatballs, 9
Sesame Salties, 6
Small Hens on the Nest, 7
Smoked Turkey or Chicken Balls, 6
Spiced Nuts, 12
Strawberry Nog, 11
Stuffed Mushrooms, 9
Wedding Punch, 11

BREADS, ROLLS, AND KUCHENS
Apple Cake, 15
Brioche Rolls, 20
Butterhorns or Nutrolls, 15
Buttermilk Rolls, 21
Caraway Bread, 20
Cinnamon Loaf, 15
Coffee Kuchen, 16
Dilly Bread, 21
Easy Cocktail Rolls, 20
Easy Danish Kringle, 17
French Doughnuts or Spritz-Krapken, 16
Hard Rolls, 21
Harvest Rolls, 21
Grandma's Oatmeal Bread, 18
Italian Bread, 18
Mary's Filled Doughnuts, 16
Mother's Depression Fruit Cake, 18
Mother's Knapf Kuchen, 18
Mother's Kranz or Wreath, 17
Mother's Muerbe Teig or Butter Pastry, 15
Orange Creme Rolls, 13
Rum Kuchen, 16

COOKING FOR A CROWD
Almond-Chicken Casserole, 59
California Chicken Salad, 59
Chili, 59
Cranberry Relish, 59
Easy-Baked Chicken, 59
Fondue, 60
German Potato Salad, 60
Ham Loaf, 60
Mint Mallow Salad, 60
Oven-Baked Chicken, 59
Spaghetti, 60

COOKING WITH EGGS
Almond Apple Pancakes, 22
Apple Omelet, 27
Baked Eggs, 27
Cheese Soufflé, 24
Fluffy Omelet, 27
Fluffy Omelet Supreme, 25
German Apple Pancake, 27
Mother's Bread Dumplings, 24
Popovers, 24
Royal Custard, 25
Sherried French Toast, 22
Soufflé Pancakes, 25
Steamed Apple Dumplings, 25
Thin Egg Pancakes—Crepes, 22
Vanilla Soufflé, 25

DESSERTS
Angel Pie, 48
Apple Nut Dessert, 52
Baked Alaska en Flambé, 56
Blitz Torte, 48
Bourbon Pound Cake, 52
Cheeseless Cheese Torte, 54
Cherry Cake Quickie, 49
Chocolate Roll, 57
Coconut Macaroon Dessert, 49
Coffee Creme Torte, 47
Coffee Log Cake, 56
Coupe Maxims, 57
Cream Cheese Torte, 54
Danish Rum Pudding, 50
Date Cake, 53
Easy Cherries Jubilee, 50
Frozen Lemon Dessert, 48
Graham Log, 53
Heavenly Pumpkin Pie, 50
Iced Zabaglione, 53
Kapazina Torte, 47
Meringues, Quick and Easy, 56
Orange Cake, 53
Peach Imperial, 48
Peach Ladyfinger Dessert, 56
Pumpkin Mallow Pie, 50
Schaum Torte, Unbaked, 54
Strawberry Macaroon Whip, 49
Thanksgiving Torte, 47
Unbaked Cheesecake, 54

MEATS
Baked Filled Chicken Breasts, 37
Beef Wellington, 32
Chicken Curry, 37
Chicken Hawaiian, 38
Frosted Meat Loaf, 32
Ground Beef Wellington, 32
Ham en Croute, 36
Ham 'N' Eggers, 36
Ham 'N' Sweets, 34
Ham Patties, 34
Ham Rollups, 36
Hens en Croute, 37
Hot Ferdinands, 34
Oven Stew, 33
Party Perfect Chicken, 38
Peach Stuffed Chicken Breasts, 38
Pepper Steak, 34
Roast Venison with Sour Cream Gravy, 37
Stuffed Hamburger Squares, 34
Swedish Meatballs, 33

SALADS
Cardinal Salad, 31
Cherry Salad, 28
Chicken Mousse, 29
Crab Meat Mold, 29
Cranberry Mold, 31
Crisp Green Salad, 28
Lemon Mold, 28
Molded Egg Salad, 31
Paradise Cranberry Salad, 31
Rice Mold, 29
Sea Dream Salad, 29
Seven Layered Salad, 28
Two-Toned Christmas Salad, 31

SEAFOOD
Baked Red Snapper, 40
Crab Quiche, 40
Flounder Rollups, 41
Salmon Pudding, 40
Seafood Casserole, 43
Seafood Soufflé, 42
Shellfish, 43
Shrimp Creole, 43
Shrimp Stroganoff, 40

VEGETABLES
Breaded Celeriac With Egg Sauce, 44
Carrot Mold, 44
Corn Fritters, 45
Crunchy Tomatoes, 44
Green Beans Caesar, 44
Spinach en Casserole, 45
Spinach Soufflé, 45
Spinach Surprise, 44

ABOUT THE AUTHOR

Gertrude Wright was a widely-recognized caterer in the Midwest for twenty-five years. For thirteen years prior to that she took courses in all aspects of cooking—nutrition, cake decorating, hotel cooking, catering, etc. Over the years, Mrs. Wright has won many awards for her work. "Imagination is the key," she says. And this creative talent has been put to use in planning hundreds of luncheons, wedding receptions and convention dinners. Many of the recipes in this cookbook were innovated during her years as a caterer; others are family favorites. Mrs. Wright is now retired and lives in Milwaukee, Wisconsin.

SX517 BOOK VIEWER STAND — The modern see-through book stand, made of strong, durable Lucite, completely protects cookbooks and other display items from smudges and dirt. The stand conveniently folds flat for easy storage or hanging. It's perfect for use in the kitchen, workshop, or home-study. A great gift idea and it's only $4.00, plus $1.00 postage and handling. Price subject to change without notice.

IDEALS RECIPE CARD BOOKLETS—Each booklet contains 32 individual 3" x 5" recipe cards, perforated for easy removal. Booklets are available in two distinctive designs and each includes a delicious easy-to-make recipe. Ideals Recipe Card Booklets may be purchased for one dollar from your local bookstore.

Editorial Director, James Kuse
Managing Editor, Ralph Luedtke
Production Editor/Manager, Richard Lawson
Photographic Editor, Gerald Koser

designed by
Debbie DuChateau

OTHER COOKBOOKS AVAILABLE

All Holidays Cookbook
American Cookbook
Christmas Cookbook
Christmas Gifts from the Kitchen
Cookie Cookbook
Country Bread Cookbook
Country Kitchen
Family Cookbook
Family Favorites from Ideals
Farmhouse Cookbook
Festive Party Cookbook
From Mama's Honey Jar
From Mama's Kitchen
Garden Cookbook
Gourmet on the Go
The Gourmet Touch
Guide to Microwave Cooking
Have a Gourmet Christmas
Junior Chef Cookbook
Menus from Around the World
Naturally Nutritious
Nice and Easy Desserts
Simply Delicious
Soups for All Seasons
Tempting Treasures
Whole Grain Cookbook

*Cover photo:
Roast Venison with
Sour Cream Gravy, p. 37*

Cover photo courtesy of the United Dairy Industry Association.